THE
MIRACLE
OF
THERAPY

THE MIRACLE OF THERAPY

A *Layperson's Guide to the Mysteries of Christian Psychology*

Georgiana G. Rodiger

WORD PUBLISHING
Dallas · London · Sydney · Singapore

The Miracle of Therapy

Copyright © 1989 by Georgiana G. Rodiger

Unless otherwise indicated, the scripture verses quoted in this book are taken from The Holy Bible, New International Version. Copyright © 1973, 1978, 1984 International Bible Society. Used by permission of Zondervan Bible Publishers. Those marked KJV are from the authorized King James Version.

Library of Congress Cataloging-in-Publication Data

Rodiger, Georgiana G., 1931–
   The miracle of therapy.

   Bibliography: p.
   1. Pastoral psychology. 2. Psychotherapy—Religious aspects—Christianity. 3. Evangelicalism. I. Title.
BV4012.R635   1989   253.5   88–33961
ISBN 0-8499-0628-8

Printed in the United States of America

9801239 BKC 987654321

To
KAY TEMPLETON
who is teaching Kingdom living
in her dying.
With courage, humor, and warmth,
she gracefully shows us the way,
the truth, and the life.

CONTENTS

FOREWORD

Georgiana Rodiger, in her exploration of the miracle of therapy, has invited us right into her office to experience firsthand what it is that makes her practice of psychotherapy so potent for so many. She takes on some of the toughest problems that therapists ever face, and by her brilliant and sparkling use of conversational reporting, she tells us precisely how she proceeded and how the "therapeutic miracle" developed.

This may well be a controversial book. She expects that. Beyond being unusually well grounded in a broad range of psychological theory and research, she maintains that her fundamental authority is a continual "listening to God with one ear and the patient with the other." Her mission is to "set the captives free," to help persons become liberated from tightly woven ways of perceiving themselves and others that have resulted in lives saturated with pain and destructiveness. If that means that she has to be blunt and dramatic and unorthodox, she never holds back. "When God directs me to speak a hard word, I have no choice," she says.

The case studies in this book are similar to an account of a world war. Each chapter represents another violent battle between the tangled and hardened intrapersonal and familial dynamics of an individual's life and the "word of God," the cutting, renewing, sometimes overwhelmingly demanding message of the gospel which guarantees genuine health, but never promises that change is easy or that it comes without intense suffering.

Georgie Rodiger is willing to stand in the middle of this kind of raging war—to help clarify the sources of twistedness and distortion and then to bring the revolutionary message that can provide dramatic healing. She seems almost impervious to the bullets that fly by her head. We might conclude that this kind of imperviousness is a fundamental requirement of therapeutic miracles.

M. Scott Peck began his classic book, *The Road Less Traveled*, with the sentence, "Life is difficult." Georgie Rodiger has brought all kinds of illumination to this simple, painful statement. She has taken us inside the lives of persons suffering from post-partum depression, marriage-threatening sexual frustrations, an inability to manage young children and older ones, eating disorders, addictions of many kinds, and the untimely death of a child. She has shown us how resistant to change persons are, especially when they are suffering. Even though their lives become enormously difficult, they often become helplessly mired in their old ways of thinking and doing. They violently resist the very change which can bring relief from their suffering.

But this book helps us to understand how positive change can occur. It is an extremely hopeful statement by a person deeply aware of reality. It maintains that God wants us to be healthy, and He will teach us how to discover this health if we will give Him a chance. When you finish this book, you are convinced that you have a choice, that you can move toward wholeness.

Nevertheless, this is not a self-help book. It does not pretend to give you a few simple answers which you can take advantage of in your spare time. Rather, it is a book about Christian psychotherapy. It tells in great detail how one therapist with a strong, Christian stance takes on persons who are stuck in a variety of painful ways.

It is fundamentally a book that teaches. It helps you understand the complex dynamics of persons who suffer from problems in living. And it teaches you about the gospel and what it has to say about these specific psychological problems. And in the process of learning about problems and solutions, you may well find yourself strangely inspired. The closer you come to the fact of a therapeutic miracle having happened in the life of a person like you, the more likely it is that a similar therapeutic miracle will happen in your own life.

NEIL CLARK WARREN

Pasadena, California
1989

INTRODUCTION

For God did not give us a spirit of timidity, but a spirit of power, of love and of self-discipline" (2 Timothy 1:7).

This book is called *The Miracle of Therapy* because in therapy miracles occur. A miracle is an extra-ordinary happening, not explicable through rational, scientific cause-and-effect reasoning. A miracle is a change we couldn't expect because it is out of the ordinary. We may hope for a miracle or even claim a miracle, as in declaring that a paralyzed child will walk, but it is always a great mystery as to when and where it will be effected. Miracles in therapy are also a great mystery because they require a number of unknown variables in the interaction between the patient and the therapist.

The constant is that God always wants to heal. His Son came among us healing all those around Him of diverse mental and physical ills. God has promised to be in our midst when "two or three come together in (His) name" (Matthew 18:20). He longs to bring us to maturity (Ephesians 4:13), to transform our minds into Christ's mind (Romans 12:2).

Therapy is an adventure in healing; recovery comes from insights, changed feelings and new behaviors. Without God's Living Power transmitted through the therapeutic hour and during the rest of the week, a patient cannot change from habitual ways of perceiving, feeling and behaving. Freed from the spirit of fear, a client gains power, the ability to love and be loved and a sound mind because God wills the miracle of transformation. The old man dies as the new creation in Christ (2 Corinthians 5:17) is born. To Him be the glory!

Life is a school of hard knocks to bring us to a realization of the only possession of true value—a relationship with God. Daily we are given opportunities to practice self-control, patience, sweet spiritedness in the face of adversity, persistence despite failures, kindness and meekness. Despite our best efforts to manage life effectively, something external or internal often throws us off balance.

We can all remember disappointments and hurts. For some, getting through each day is very difficult. The job, the family, the adult toys, even recreational activities cease to give pleasure. Others have suffered a grievous loss through death, divorce, a diagnosis of progressive illness, a move away from loved ones, or suddenly being unemployed.

No matter how hard we try, we run into brick walls. Carefully picking ourselves up, checking for broken bones, dusting ourselves off, we vow we'll never let that catastrophe overtake us again. Diligently we plan for future success, trying to anticipate any impediments along the way. All goes well for awhile and we settle into self-satisfaction. We've figured out how to live. We don't need anyone's help. *Those poor slobs who keep getting into difficulties*, we think to ourselves, *should seek our advice on parenting, interpersonal relationships, employment, self-management and the spiritual life.*

Then, when we least expect it, the brick wall rises in our own path. We smash into it again. Smug belief in the capacity to manage ourselves lies in the dust around us. "Unfair!" we shout. "We haven't done anything to deserve this setback," we complain. "Why did I get cancer? I'm too young to die," we moan. "My child can't be flunking first grade!" "My boss couldn't be firing me!" "It's not right!" "God must be asleep, letting all these bad things happen to me!"

We moan and groan and complain because life doesn't work out the way we expect. We feel cheated, unhappy, unappreciated; we begin to lose our motivation to keep going. Depression and bitterness often are the aftermath of repeated wall bumping. It gets harder and harder to hope things will work out. Even faith in God is often shaken. He should have kept the children from getting hurt in the automobile accident. He should have rewarded faithful service on the job with a promotion instead of a layoff.

Very few people come into therapy just to learn about themselves or examine their lives. Some do and find that therapy is a more exciting and rewarding exploration than a trip around the world. Investigating the unknown parts of ourselves, called the unconscious, is like entering a great underground cave full of hidden treasures. The flashlight of insight illuminates sparkling gems, secret passages, small lakes, soaring chambers, hidden wonders. Many people *continue* in therapy for the excitement of ongoing growth, but they *start* because they've hit a wall.

The Last Resort

Most individuals seeking therapy want change. The problems that brought them to a mental health professional make life uncomfortable, if not unbearable. The therapist is a last resort; most people would prefer to visit the dentist. To admit we have a problem managing our lives is very humiliating. Relief from symptoms is the spur that pushes a client into making the first call. Then, the appointment made, anxiety increases until, with sweating palms and pounding heart, the moment of first contact arrives. Hope alternates with doubt as the conversation begins. *Can this doctor really help me? Will I be able to explain clearly what's bothering me? Will he think I'm stupid because I haven't been able to think through a solution? Will he feel I'm foolish for not having been able to change my behavior? Will I have to share embarrassing details about my life? Will the doctor lecture, as some of my friends have lectured, or give advice I can't seem to use? Will he be shocked by what I have done or how I think?*

These, and many other questions, rush frantically through a client's head as he presents himself for therapy. It takes real courage to keep that first appointment, as anyone who has taken this step knows. And it costs real money, hard-earned dollars. Somehow, paying for talking seems unfair!

We all talk to each other all the time. Why does talking to this stranger cost an arm and a leg? Does he really know how to deal with my kind of trouble? Maybe I'm just wasting my time and money. It's hard to schedule in weekly appointments; my time is already squeezed between work and family responsibilities. Is my life so uncomfortable or so unfulfilled that I must move into the great unknown? What skills do I need to be a good client? What stress or discomfort will I undergo? Will I emerge with all my abilities intact? Is the expense and the risk really worth it? I've listened to the tales of those who have gone through therapy, and I've read books about the process. But can I trust those others? Would my experience be comparable? Have I chosen the right therapist for my kind of problem?

There are many different kinds of therapists and a variety of systems. In dentistry, at least, presumably filling a cavity is filling a cavity. Any trained, licensed dentist can diagnose and treat a sore tooth. However, unraveling the mysteries of human behavior is a far more complicated business. Many paths are available; many guides promise health and comfort.

Gurus shout from radios and television sets: "I know how to make you happy, wealthy, thin, sexual, successful." Magazines contain articles about problems and how to solve them according to an expert in the field of mental health. Books filled with promises come out daily and are popular best sellers. Many of them denigrate other systems' ideas and interventions.

It is a bewildering maze. Dire consequences are foretold for the unwary who trust in the wrong therapist. Everyone hears of clients who have been in treatment for years, spending thousands of dollars, and are worse off than they were before they began. Psychiatric horror stories get big headlines suggesting futility, if not danger, for those who embark upon the adventure of psychological growth.

Church-centered Terror

For Christians, it's even worse. Some churches teach that healing for mental pain is appropriately sought only through prayer, fasting and the laying on of hands. To go into therapy is considered sinful, a cause for chastisement from the pastor and embarrassment within the congregation. If a person seeks professional mental help, he may be asked to resign his membership.

John

John came to see me because his physician suggested he consult a psychologist to alleviate recurrent severe headaches. Elaborate medical tests had ascertained that nothing was physically wrong, suggesting a psychological cause for his pain. John's ability to work was suffering, as well as his capacity to meet the needs of his wife and children.

Seldom have I seen a more terrified man. He had insisted on an appointment after dark and told me he would pay in cash. When he called to schedule the appointment, he asked me not to record his name in my book, just his initials; and he questioned whether I needed to jot down information. I assured him I would not write anything down nor open a file. Then he asked if I knew anyone from a particular church fifty miles away from my office. Reassured by my negative response, John appeared at the appointed hour, looking furtively around at others in the waiting room. As I ushered him into my office, he pressed cash into my hand and told me he had parked his car several blocks away. He apologized for these elaborate precautions, explaining a story now familiar to me about a pastor who forbade his flock to seek psychological counsel on pain of hellfire preceded by excommunication.

"Psychology is of the Devil; marriage and family counselors deliberately lead people away from God's Word; therapists invade your thinking as the Devil invaded Eve's thinking; God is sufficient for all our needs without any interventions except prayer and fasting!" thundered from the pulpit every Sunday morning.

I asked John if his pastor was equally opposed to medical consultations or surgical interventions. Nervously, he replied that his pastor believed God used those doctors when necessary for healing; only mental health professionals were identified as belonging to the Prince of Darkness. He was frankly terrified of the magical power he believed I possessed; but he was equally terrified of the imminent loss of his ability to support his family if the headaches persisted.

I was privileged to attend a seminary that realized the necessity for Christians to understand human behavior and learn how to set captives free from psychological bondage. Fuller Theological Seminary in Pasadena, California, established a School of Psychology, and a Marriage, Family, and Child Counseling Program in the late 1960s, despite violent disagreement from some of their conservative supporters. It was a bold move; opposition ran high. They pressed on bravely into new territory, establishing the finest school in the world for educating Christian mental health professionals.

As a student at Fuller from 1973 to 1980, I was deeply moved by being part of the intensive effort the Seminary expended in studying the integration of theological and behavioral truths. Adhering strictly to the Scriptures, the students and faculty hammered out a Christian understanding of psychological discoveries. We discussed every kind of intrapsychic and external problem possible on life's journey, exploring ways to give sight to the blind and freedom to the captive. What a joyous time that was—praying and studying with bright men and women who loved the Lord!

So when John nervously sought my help, I was able to assure him that I was not in the employ of Satan, nor did I have magic powers. Mental health professionals are guides, trained to bring seekers through the wilderness. With the help of the Holy Spirit, I could ascertain if there were psychological reasons for John's problems. We are trained to know the language of the unconscious, and to help him find more adequate tools to manage himself in daily living and stress-filled situations. I wouldn't take control of his life (God is our Lord and Master) or teach him anything that was not scripturally based.

John was astonished. He asked how a pastor so learned and sound in other matters could be misinformed about therapy. I replied, "To the best of my understanding, I believe it is because Freud thought God was a projection of the unconscious, and Watson believed that scientific methodology required leaving the unmeasurable out of the equation. Older pastors may not have been exposed to the writings of Christian psychologists and psychologically knowledgeable Christians."

Anguished Questions

This book is written for my friends who have asked for a guide to the mysteries of Christian psychology. Not having been privileged to share the seven-year dialogue I enjoyed at Fuller, they have asked me many questions: "What is therapy? How does it work? How do I choose the right therapist? How do I know if he's helping me? Why won't God heal me directly? Why does He let me suffer? If I explore my unconscious, will I discover facts about myself that will make me feel guilty? Will I become angry and then be rude to my parents, wife, co-workers? Do I have to confront those who have hurt me and make them feel badly? If I go into therapy will I lose my drive to succeed, my artistic talents, my search for passion in my life? Should I just accept my emotionally crippled life as God's will? Does He want me never to have friends or make an adequate living? What does He want us to learn about our sinfulness through the agony of our child's dying? Does He want our developmentally disabled child to stay handicapped? Is our inability to enjoy each other sexually our punishment for having made love before we got married? Am I depressed because I masturbated as a teenager? Is our daughter's anorexia God's judgment on us because we occasionally miss church? My father hates my husband; how have I failed?"

This book is written to give insights into how one Christian therapist thinks about these presenting problems and many others. It is made up of case histories, compiled from the patients I have seen in twelve years of practice. These particular stories illustrate some of the problems mental health professionals may be called to explore.

In the beginning of each chapter, I will give a short introduction to the case material. As the work unfolds, I will share what we discovered about the unconscious conflicts. A summary of the material and relevant psychological and theological concepts will end the chapter.

Junior

I call the part of ourselves which controls most of our thoughts, feelings and behaviors "Junior," or "the unconscious." No one who is comfortable with all his feelings and behaviors comes to talk to a therapist. I understand my task to be discovering the way a client's Junior sabotages his good intentions and desired thoughts. Saint Paul said, "I do not understand what I do. For what I want to do, I do not do, but what I hate I do" (Romans 7:15).

We study Junior's values, beliefs, and desires through talking about what the client has done during the week, how he felt and what he dreamt. A good client learns to talk about his daily life, and to notice unusual thoughts, feelings, and actions. He remembers dreams. As we carefully scrutinize this material, the client and I become more and more aware of the "little one" inside. Junior is often no more than two or three years old. If you think about the two-year-olds you have known, it becomes obvious why bad habits and thought patterns are hard to break. Two-year-olds are opinionated, stubborn, oppositional, selfish and intensely involved with their feelings. When angry, they have temper tantrums; when pleased, they are filled with hugs and kisses.

By thirty-six months of age, all of us have learned a great deal about the nature of reality and interpersonal relationships. If our mothers have been available to us for most of every day and our households relatively free from tension, we feel comfortable in the world and in relationships. A well-nurtured three-year-old likes himself so well he is convinced others should do things his way. He has learned the rules about eating, bedtime, bath, car trips, shopping, gifts, Sunday school, grandparents, toys, parks, animals, television, swimming pools, flowers, breakable objects, knives, etc. He knows he is loved unequivocally. The love God has for people is transmitted to the young child through the unconditional affection of his parents. He is able to stand up to giants (adults) and say "No, not those jammies," "Give me a lollipop," "I hate you, you're a bad mommy," and "I love you."

Securely grounded, the child can attend to learning how objects and relationships function in the world. He feels the difference between throwing a glass or a ball, or between hugging a cat or a snail. He experiences hitting a parent or biting another child. He observes the relationships between parents and children, lovers, siblings, pastors and people, grandparents, dogs and postmen. If the child continues to be in a safe environment with loving adults, he learns by watching and experimenting with the way the world works; he begins to understand people's feelings. He enjoys his capacities and accepts his failings. Learning in school and on the playground comes easily because his anxiety is minimal.

For most of the people we see in therapy, the above was not the scenario. When they were little, their parents were stressed because of family, financial, or personal problems. Their homes were full of tension or fighting. Sometimes they were severely scolded for misusing or breaking objects, often producing in the adult a timid approach to experiences in the world. Frequently they were left for long periods every day with strangers, babysitters, or daycare workers, resulting in abandonment fears and disturbed love relationships as adults. These and other developmental antecedents will be discussed in this book. Buried deep inside many of us, carefully shielded from the conscious mind, is a loving, raging infant with faulty perceptions about the true nature of reality. The task of the therapist is to be a guide for the client, encouraging each step, as they explore infantile feelings and beliefs.

There are expected thrills and obstacles for the therapeutic voyager. Junior's opinions and desires are often not acceptable to the adult person sitting before me so the patient blocks them out of his awareness. For example, the child who substituted cookies for her absent mother, filling herself with sweets to fill the aching void, may find dieting difficult as an adult despite extensive nutritional information. The reason she cannot lose weight is centered much more in Junior's needs that produce compulsive overeating, than in her adult decisions.

The man who quits his job each time he begins to be promoted and paid adequately may be driven by an unconscious fear of losing his dad if he achieves success, due to a faulty connection between his academic success in kindergarten and his parents' divorce. We know his competence did not cause the marital breakup, but his "little mind" put two and two together and came up with five.

Journeying together, the patient and the clinician explore the unconscious. When familiar landmarks appear, they can understand why the woman eats or the man quits. He or she can then learn other ways to deal with the conflict arising from early experiences.

Understanding Personalities

A further word about the makeup of human personality might be in order as a point of reference for the discussions in each of the chapters. Imagine, if you will, a triangle pointing upward. Then draw two horizontal lines through the center. This is the repression barrier. In it are the ego defenses. Label the upper line *thinking* and the lower line *feeling.* In the top point of the triangle write *Conscious Ego* (CE). Below the two lines write *Unconscious*

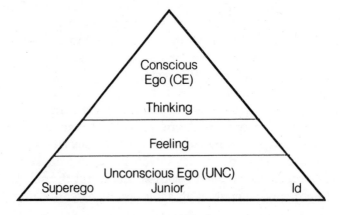

Ego (UNC) or *Junior*. *Superego* and *Id* go in the left and right lower corners respectively.

Now picture, if you will, a battle going on most of the time between the superego and the id in the bottom of our triangle. The id says, "I want to eat a dozen donuts"; and the superego says, "You'll get fat." The id says, "I want to play all day"; the superego says, "You have to support your family." The conscious ego's job (the top of the triangle) is to deal with the world and get on with daily living. He cannot spend time and energy attending to the battle; he blocks it out of his mind. This is called *repression*. He pushes it down below the two lines and is unaware it is going on at all. Some people are more able to do this than others. Psychotics—so-called crazy people—can't do it at all; others have major difficulties repressing uncomfortable material.

Repression is a defense. It defends the person from having to think about (cognition) or feel (affect) the battle between the superego and the id. There are a number of other defenses. For example, instead of feeling rage at a mother who wasn't really there for Junior, a woman might get very involved in La Leche League, teaching new mothers to be available to their infants through long-term breastfeeding. That's the defense of *sublimation*. Or she might become a research psychologist and study the bonding needs of infants, including hours of observations on mother-baby interactions. That is the defense of *intellectualization*, defending against the pain of longing for mother by understanding the dyadic (bonding) relationship.

Rather than stand the distress of hearing parents' arguing all the time, a child might develop asthma. Each asthmatic attack would stop the fights as both parents rush to help their suffocating youngster. Careful tracking by a trained specialist linking asthma attacks with family fights might indicate a psychological as well as a physical origin. This is the defense of *somatization*.

Other defenses will be discussed in the case histories. Of course, my simplistic model of a human being as a triangle is only a tool to help us understand unconscious conflicts and defenses. The battle between our basic wishes for immediate comfort and our parents', teachers', or bosses' voices within us saying, "Get to work," "You'll get fat," "Save for tomorrow," "Be kind," and many other injunctions never stops during our lifetime. We can use more sophisticated defenses once we have insight into why we do what we do, but we can never quiet the inner battle completely.

Abba, Father

Into this lifelong task our God comes bringing forgiveness and the peace that passes understanding. What that means is that His peace is able to quiet the internal wrangling as He calmed the storm. He made us and lived here, in the person of Jesus, so He knows what we experience. He is our Comforter, the Rock upon which we stand.

As a Christian therapist, I know that our God reigns. He has dominion over all conflict and darkness; His light illumines our struggles; His Word informs our words. I know the darkest hour comes just before the dawn. The worst pain can be borne by those formed in God's image and likeness; the cruelest conflicts can be resolved because Jesus is the Great Mediator. As a guide through the wilderness of each person's unique history and problems, I know that the Land of Milk and Honey can be reached by those who go forward despite intrapsychic pain and fear. It can be uncomfortable to search our unconscious and find our inappropriate defenses. The reward is entering into the Promised Land.

Therapists give new perspectives, just as God called people throughout the Scriptures to see events in a new way. Abraham's descendants are numbered as the stars because of his obedience, not because of the miracle of Isaac's birth to a ninety-year-old woman. If Abraham had believed Isaac was the key to the promise, he would never have prepared to sacrifice him. Moses knew a Land of Milk and Honey was awaiting the children of Israel. If he had lost faith as the months became years, the people would have been without a guide. Even his relative and spokesman before the Pharaoh, Aaron, succumbed to the people's fear, creating for them a golden calf, a false defense to be idolized.

If Jesus had accepted the prevailing cultural mores regarding the oldest son's duty to help his widowed mother with the younger children, the greatest life ever lived and most precious death ever died would not have happened. The Bible is a book of unexpected perspectives lived out in obedience to God's will, not man's common sense or institutionalized rules. Therapy must provide new visions of God's will in men's and women's lives.

Hitting the wall, I believe, is part of God's plan for our lives in this school of hard knocks called life. He doesn't send trouble, but He allows the Prince of Darkness to roam freely in the world, causing disharmony and tragedy. Flat in the dust we are given the opportunity with Job to say, "Even though He slay me, yet will I hope in him" (Job 13:15). Without hardships and disappointments, we become complacent, convinced we can manage our own lives. Only from our humble awareness of impotence can we truly cry, "Abba, Father."

Several details needing clarification must be addressed as I finish this introduction. Two diagrams, a glossary, and a bibliography are included in the appendix to assist the reader who is unfamiliar with some of the language used in the text. The labels *client* and *patient* will be used interchangeably. Existential-humanistic psychologists prefer *client* to get away from the medical model prevalent in older psychoanalytic usage. Here at the Rodiger Center, we use a variety of therapies, selecting the ones most appropriate for each client/patient. The pronoun *he* will always be used unless I am referring to a woman or girl. With all due respect to the women's liberation position on sexist language, I find reading easier if conventional use of pronouns is followed.

Many of the clients seen at the Rodiger Center are not Christians. It is our ethical responsibility to work with them within the parameters of their value systems, and not to try to convert them to ours. We are absolutely forbidden to evangelize those who come to us for therapy. We use Christian terminology with those who speak that language, and secular psychological terminology with those who don't.

The stories in this book are composites of clients seen in private practice, in group sessions, and in workshops. All case histories have been modified (with the exception of "Philip") so that the anonymity of those who have so generously shared their most private thoughts and feelings will be protected. The cases vary widely to give the reader as broad an experience of the ways God works through psychology as possible.

Writing this book will have been worthwhile if you, the reader, are inspired to leave the safety of your comfortable habits and thought patterns to seek the richer land God has planned for you.

I want to thank all the patients who have shared their lives with me. Through their courage and hard work I have been privileged to experience the fascinating intricacy and awesome grandeur of the creature made "a little lower than the heavenly beings and crowned with glory and honor" (Psalm 8:5). Doing therapy feels like reaching inside another person and touching the face of God.

My deepest appreciation to my mentor and friend, Dr. Warren Jones, who shared his wisdom and professional expertise, making this book possible. My gratitude also goes to Dr. Aune Strom, who buried herself in tomes at the Fuller library compiling my glossary and bibliography. My profoundest thanks go to Shirley Cox, who typed and retyped this manuscript, miraculously never giving up on me when client hours and family matters constantly interfered with the completion of this project. She is one of God's most patient saints!

1

It's Fun to Be Sane

JEANIE

Synopsis: Jeanie and Pete came to see me because of her severe postpartum depression. The psychiatrist recommended that Jeanie be hospitalized, but she wanted to continue nursing Alison. Jeanie discovered, through therapy, that she had resented her younger brother and sisters and had absorbed her mother's severe anxiety.

Through cognitive behavior modification, daily intensive physical exercise, and directed readings, Jeanie was able to control her obsessive thinking. The unconscious conflicts, defended against by obsessions and panic attacks, were a strong desire to get rid of her baby brother and sisters now projected onto Alison, and jealousy over her mother's seeming to prefer her newborn babies over her firstborn, Jeanie. That jealousy was projected onto Pete with baby Alison.

As Jeanie developed self-management skills, she was able to stop looking to Pete to make her happy, as her mother had looked to her father. She learned to contain her emotions so she could give Alison a calm mother. Her expectations of Pete had changed dramatically by their last visit, when Alison was fourteen months old.

It's Fun to Be Sane

Jeanie and her husband Pete came to me when their baby was only ten days old. Jeanie's psychiatrist had said she was suffering from such severe postpartum depression that she needed to be heavily medicated in a psychiatric facility. Jeanie and Pete were both born-again Christians from dedicated families.

They hoped there was some way to avoid hospitalization so that Jeanie could continue to nurse little Alison. Jeanie said she was frantic; she felt as though she were jumping out of her skin. She was terrified of everything and insisted that Pete stay home from work to keep her company. She couldn't go out of the house. She couldn't sleep. She couldn't eat. The good news was that she could nurse Alison. She had plenty of milk and Alison sucked lustily.

As the little one lay in her mother's arms, I shuddered to consider the effect on her of being abandoned for a month at this point in her life. For her, the bonding would be disrupted; never again could Alison believe that the world was totally trustworthy, that the everlasting arms would hold her. A baby is born with a need as strong as its need for food, to be bonded to its mother. If its mother is not available, it will bond to another person. That person is crucial for the first two years of a baby's life. All kinds of difficulties result if a baby doesn't have unlimited access day and night to its mother or to a mothering person.

Of course, many babies survive despite disruptions in bonding. We often see them later as anxious children with learning disabilities, hyperactivity or various diseases like asthma and eczema. As adults they fill the psychologists' waiting rooms. An infant learns who he is through the mirroring of his mother's hands and eyes. He develops a strong sense of himself as a unique, valuable human being because his mother sends him that message through the hours they spend together. For Alison, hospitalization of her mother could be disastrous.

I asked Pete and Jeanie when these panic attacks first began. They remembered her periodically becoming frantically anxious. However, most of the time after the pregnancy started to show, she was able to continue working as a buyer in a women's clothing store. It hadn't occurred to them that she might become incapacitated after the birth.

No one at Pete's work could understand why his wife couldn't be left alone for eight hours of the day with the baby. He didn't know either, but he could feel her terror. Soon he had to get back to work as a wholesale distributor of sporting goods.

Jeanie and Pete had been married for six years. Jeanie was now thirty-six years of age and they both had longed for this infant to start their family. They were puzzled by this turn of events, as was the psychiatrist. The little baby was healthy and beautiful, a perfect infant.

I asked Jeanie about her childhood. She was the first child. Three years later, a boy was born and, shortly thereafter, two girls joined the family. She remembered her mother's constant anxiety about their health and well-being. Jeanie recalled endless admonishments not to climb, not to run, not to fall, not to eat certain things because they would make her sick, and to be careful about cuts and bruises because they might turn toxic. She was deluged by a daily litany of danger in a fearful world. "Even today," Jeanie said, laughing, "when I speak to my mother, she responds to anything I say with 'Be careful!' or 'Look out!' or 'It might not work out' or 'It sounds too risky.'"

That laugh gave me hope. I commented, "It sounds as if you've been able to manage the anxiety your mother telegraphed to you through all your years of growing up relatively well by being a successful professional. But now that you've given birth to a helpless infant, you're being overwhelmed by fear." She agreed.

I asked Jeanie if she knew what the first recorded words were when Jesus was born. She was a good church member and with a little thought she recalled that the angels had said to the shepherds, "Fear not." I said, "Our God reigns. Since He came to earth and became one of us, we do not have any reason to be afraid. Death has no dominion! Difficulties and tragedies can be surmounted because God is on our side. His Comforter will keep us in perfect peace."

"Your mother didn't take responsibility for containing this world's anxieties to give you children a free space in which to grow. Daily upsets, worries, and fears were shared physically and verbally with all of you."

"Yes, that's true. My brothers and sisters are pretty uptight individuals, too."

"Grownups know that bad things can happen, but they keep anxiety to themselves," I told Jeanie. "Even on the Nazis' cattle cars going to Dachau, the mature grownups continued to tell stories to calm the children. Fears about the stability of the world and the possibility of the maiming or death of a child are contained by most adults, so children can attend to their business, which is learning and growing."

After a pause, Jeanie commented, "My mother still doesn't contain any of her fears."

"Now, with the birth of Alison, you can become your mother."

"Heaven forbid!" she exclaimed.

"Good idea. Heaven will forbid it if you'll ask Heaven, God Himself, to give you the courage to be a grownup," I suggested.

Jeanie agreed to pray.

I asked how she felt when her brother and sisters were born.

"I can't remember. I was too little. My youngest sister was born when I was only six."

"Okay, try to imagine how you must have felt. You were a little girl, going to school learning to read and write while at home your mother is in a frenzy of anxiety, caring for two toddlers and an infant. How do you think you felt?"

After sitting quietly for a moment, Jeanie replied, "Well, I don't know. I tried very hard to help her take care of them. I remember that."

"I'm sure that's true; but I think, underneath, you were pretty angry that she'd saddled your young life with so much responsibility. I bet you babysat with them and tried to help your mother manage her anxiety so she could keep the household running. In fact, I think you often wished that they weren't there, that she had been content to have you as her only child."

"Gosh, I never thought of that!" exclaimed Jeanie.

"To go into a major panic reaction as you have, because what you're suffering from is much more severe than just postpartum depression, suggests an unconscious component," I told her. "I think the unconscious component is that you're not at all sure you want to share your husband's love with this interloper Alison. Pete's the person you look to for emotional support."

"Heavens, it doesn't occur to me consciously that Alison is a rival for Pete's attention!" she responded.

We both looked where Pete was happily playing with the baby, enchanted with his infant daughter. Everything in his face quickened as he contemplated her miniature face and tiny hands. He was the very picture of a doting lover.

I asked Jeanie, "When was the last time Pete looked at you like that?"

She grinned ruefully. "Well, not for a long time. He paid a great deal of attention when we were first married but now we're sort of good friends rather than feeling very much romantic excitement. I really miss being close."

Controlling Junior's Rage

I explained that I could really imagine how her mother, looking at each baby when they were tiny with fascinated eyes, had produced in Jeanie, as a little girl, a stab of such fierce jealousy and rage that she wished the infants were dead. Now those primitive emotions were rising up from Junior and threatening to unbalance her mind.

Jeanie asked, "How can I keep my mind calm? I worry all the time that Alison will get sick or hurt because I'm not watching closely enough."

I said, "Walk! Put the baby on your chest in a little pack and get out and walk at least four hours a day, preferably six."

"When can I do my housework?"

"Don't bother. Ignore the housework if you're too tired after all that walking to dust and vacuum. Your husband will do it or he'll walk the baby on Saturday so that you'll have a few hours to attend to the house. Furthermore, never separate Alison from your body. Always have her right next to you. When the baby sleeps, you sleep. When the baby plays, you play. When the baby's nursing, you relax and enjoy looking at her lovely little face. No phone calls, no meetings, no planning next fall's fashion show. Do nothing except enjoy your infant."

She asked, "May I go walk at the mall?"

"Sure, for one of those four hours, but the other three, I want you to walk fast, up and down the streets of Los Angeles."

"How can I stay asleep at night? I keep waking up?"

"Don't bother. Get a good novel, and plan to read all night. Sooner or later, you'll doze off. Your body is perfectly self-regulatory, if you'll stop worrying."

Jeanie sighed. "I feel much better right now. But I know that as soon as I leave you and go home, the terror will begin."

"It will try to begin," I said. "But you'll put the baby on your chest and walk right out the door, smiling sweetly at Pete as you leave."

Nervously, she asked, "Pete can't come?"

"Certainly not. Pete has to go to work tomorrow. The family's bread and butter depends on Pete's labor and he cannot take any more time off. You walk through the city streets with your baby by yourself, four hours a day. I want you to call me every night at nine to tell me how your day went."

She was startled. "I never heard of a doctor who talked on the phone to her patient every day!"

"I know that the infant inside you is the one who is causing the panic attacks. Junior hasn't the capacity to remember anything for more than twenty-four hours, because she's so young. The reassurance you're presently feeling will be gone in twenty-four hours so you'll need to talk to me tomorrow night. You want to nurse the baby; that means no pills and no hospital. Babies can't tolerate psychotropic medication. You know that you're as safe as any other human being in this nuclear age and that you want all the best for Alison. It's Junior who's giving us static! There isn't any way I can see you once a week and keep your anxiety at a manageable level."

Pete said, sadly, "We can't even afford to see you once a week. We don't have any money now that Jeanie had to stop working. She always brought in the lion's share of our income, but I really feel strongly she needs to stay home with the baby for at least three months."

I spoke forcefully. "For at least two years, even if it means selling the house! A mother must be with her infant for at least two years."

Pete agreed. "We must afford therapy, or Jeanie may end up in the mental hospital. But we don't have the money to pay your fee."

"You can borrow money against your house. Jeanie's mental health is crucial. Alison needs a cheerful mother now more than future financial security."

Jeanie and Alison came to see me every week. Pete went back to work and Jeanie walked to control her panic. For a month, we talked every night on the phone. Alison thrived at the breast, becoming a round, cheerful baby.

Every time Jeanie expressed a fear to me, I asked whether worrying about that particular possibility was worth giving up nursing to go to a psychiatric institution.

Each time she'd reply, "Absolutely not."

Then I'd say, "Well, then why bother to worry? Of course, that might happen, but it might not. Disengage your brain from those obsessive thoughts."

It was very hard work. If you've never been an obsessive person, I can't possibly describe to you how difficult it is to block neuronal pathways that are grooved deeply in childhood. Remember what it felt like when you were in high school and had fallen in love with the captain of the football team? Your days and your nights were consumed with thoughts of his perfection and how much fun you two would have together. Every nuance of conversation that did occur between you was analyzed and reanalyzed. Possibilities that might come from that relationship in the future were minutely scrutinized. Waking and sleeping, your mind was consumed with the love object. So it is for the person with an obsession.

Jeanie had a long up-hill battle. She needed constant reassurance that she was an adequate mother, that Alison was doing well, that she did not need to worry. She knew it with her adult persona, but Junior screamed, "Look out!", "Be careful!", "The world is a dangerous place!" All of her mother's old sayings had been grooved deeply in her brain at a very impressionable age.

A Different Way to Be Born Again

In theological terms it might be said that Jeanie was called to be born again—not in the way some evangelical Christians use that term, but in the sense of having her mind transformed. The "old man," the old automatic ways of being, had to be shed. She was as fragile and vulnerable during that process as a baby chick just out of the shell. Being born again does not mean getting back inside one's mother's womb as Nicodemus imagined. It means reforming the habitual structures of our brains as completely as if we were once again being introduced for the first time to this world. That's extremely difficult to do. Most people don't have the courage to try. Jeanie wouldn't have dared to change her habitual ways of thinking, her fearful attitude toward life, were it not for a little person called Alison. God in His great wisdom sent Alison to Jeanie, allowed her to feel the panic attacks, and then sent her to me.

As God's mouthpiece, my job is to speak His healing Word. Having left us bodily, He sent His Holy Spirit to dwell inside us, closer to our minds and hearts than He Himself could be while on earth. We speak a Spirit-directed healing Word to one another. I believe God arranged a sequence of events to expose Jeanie's pathology and then to heal it.

Jeanie could have gone into a psychiatric hospital, and put Alison on the bottle. The disrupted bonding would have produced frequent irritation at the demanding little person, just as she had been irritated by her little siblings. Before long, she would have decided that she needed to go back to work to contain her anxiety. She had good control over the clothing purchased for her store. The world seemed orderly and measurable from the point of view of a fashion buyer's desk.

Instead, Jeanie chose the hard course. Under my guidance, she began to allow God to reform her into His image and likeness. She began to put on the "mind of Christ" (1 Corinthians 2:16).

"Therefore I tell you, do not worry about your life" (Matthew 6:25). "Do not let your hearts be troubled" (John 14:1). She became a little child for Christ's sake.

For a long time Jeanie was like two people: one playing the old tapes, and one wrestling in desperate combat to maintain her sanity. She could feel the two parts of herself talking to each other. She wondered if this was schizophrenia, having read the popular literature that suggested schizophrenia meant dual personality. I assured her that it was not. She was simply being transformed, a 180-degree change brought about through repentance and a desire to lead a new life following the commandments of God and walking in His ways.

It was a horrendous struggle, fought hourly in the beginning. Slowly the hard exercise and the obviously flourishing infant began to drive her automatic panic reactions away. It was hard to be frightened on a beautiful morning when she was walking briskly down familiar streets with a lovely infant asleep on her chest. After a month, we stopped talking to each other every evening. She knew my number and was free to call me if needed. We continued to see each other in therapy, once a week.

The next question we addressed was why she didn't have a better relationship with Pete. They were living as good companions but they were not intensely involved emotionally. Like a brother and sister, they were comfortable together. Jeanie wanted more. One day she asked about bringing Pete in to revive the closeness of their relationship.

I asked, "Why do you want an intense, romantic relationship with Pete?"

She looked startled and replied, "Well, from everything I read, I gather that's what marriage is all about."

I grinned. "You read the wrong magazines and I bet you enjoy romantic novels."

It was her turn to smile and look a little sheepish. "Harlequin novels are my favorite."

I suggested she consider looking at the books of some of the wise people written in past centuries to get a better perspective on how they attained peace and joy in this world. I suggested she study the life of Jesus to see where He gained His strength and sagacity.

Jeanie came back the next week and asked me if I was suggesting that a person shouldn't expect other people to keep them happy.

I replied, "Right on!"

"But my mom always told my dad that it was his responsibility to solve her problems and keep her feeling cheerful."

"Did he accomplish that assignment?"

"No," Jeanie replied. "He was never adequate. She repeatedly said so. My mother told my dad that if he were a better man she wouldn't feel so awful all the time."

"I think that's wicked. Your poor father, years and years and years of being made to feel inadequate because every time something upset your mother, and it sounds as if everything upset your mother, somehow it became his problem. I also feel sorry for your mother. She never, in all of her fifty-eight years, has taken responsibility for her own centeredness, her own balance in life, the management of her own feelings. Instead, she looks to your dad to give her peace. God is the great Comforter. As long as we're looking to another person to take care of us and make us feel better, there is no way God can get through. We are called to rely solely on God as our best friend, to passionately pursue our relationship with Him. Then we can enjoy our husbands, children, friends, parents, and companions at work."

Accepting Responsibility

For Alison's sake, Jeanie studied how to be responsible for herself. When she began to go off balance, she figured out what she could do to remediate that situation. Sometimes, there was more exercise. Sometimes, it was a nice cool glass of iced tea. Sometimes, it was reading the Bible, praying or painting. Sometimes, it was writing a poem. I urged her not to turn on television, which usually talks about relationships at a very moronic level. The commercials increase tension with fast words and jumpy music so that we'll buy their products. I suggested she immerse herself in writers such as C. S. Lewis, Madeleine

L'Engle, William Stringfellow, John Stott, and, of course, the Bible, rather than read romantic novels.

Jeanie was astonished to discover how little the Bible said about feelings. She noticed that Jesus never sat down and had a conversation with His disciples about how He felt. His feelings were expressed through His actions. He owned them and He acted on them. She noticed that that was true of the people in the Old Testament as well as the New. She asked why experiencing feelings and communicating them had become such a major preoccupation in modern American society.

I explained that feelings had only been a national preoccupation in the last thirty years. During the sixties and seventies, because the country was experiencing a rapidly expanding economy and our wars were limited, many people had the leisure to become concerned about how they felt and interacted with others.

The contemplation of one's emotions and relationships with other people has always been possible for those who don't have to work. Robert Coles, a Harvard professor and a Christian, has written a number of books about children of different ethnic and socioeconomic backgrounds. One of his books is called *The Privileged Ones*. In it he describes the particular training that goes on in America for the children of the rich, who will always be able to afford more leisure than the average person. He points out that they are given a very specific, intensive set of experiences, nannies, boarding school and summer camps, to teach them how to use leisure time. They are taught to contain emotions.

The worst possible show of bad manners for the upper classes is the display of feelings. Overreactions to tragedy or achievements are considered in very poor taste. This is drilled into them by their governesses and school teachers from their youth. It is expected that in the midst of profound grief, such as losing a husband, they will maintain their composure and, in times of triumph, such as being inaugurated President of the United States, they will deport themselves with equanimity.

Think, if you will, of the picture of Jackie Kennedy and her two children as the President's hearse rolled by. Think of Winston Churchill in the darkest hours of England, maintaining sufficient composure to inspire his countrymen with ringing words. Think of Franklin Roosevelt, paralyzed from the waist down, keeping his big smile and capacity to carry crushing burdens. Think of the Queen of England. Can you imagine seeing her become hysterical and frantic over anything? This is training, begun in early child-hood and maintained by social pressure among the elite.

The United States government has shown, in a study done in 1985 with five thousand people, that adults who contain their anger are healthier than those who express it. Yet magazine articles and pop psychology books still encourage wives to tell their husbands exactly how they feel when they come home from work. It's no wonder many men dread going home. They are urged to communicate what they are thinking but if they share financial worries or outside interests, some women get very upset.

Nothing is more frightening to children than grownups whose emotions are mercurial. They never know whether mother is going to be calm and cheerful or exploding in tearful rage. The slightest thing sets her off; their world rocks. Little children have no way to control the daily occurrences which so unhinge their mothers. They have to make the best of it. Their capacity to attend to their learning is severely damaged because they spend so much time trying to keep mother stable.

Pete was exhausted from financial responsibility and the stress at home. He simply couldn't give any more. Jeanie wanted to grow into a whole—holy—person. She decided not to expect Pete's support or appreciation; she wanted to enjoy Pete for himself. Agape love means that we love another because they are there, not because they meet any of our needs.

The last time I saw Jeanie, she was calm and poised. I couldn't believe the contrast in her present appearance from our first visit. Pete was delighted with Jeanie's growth. Alison was fourteen months old, a perfect toddler. She was bright and curious, walking well, into everything. Every day Jeanie had to deal with her internal dynamics. Because she wanted the best for Alison, she allowed the Lord to use the baby to transform her. Jeanie had begun to really understand what it meant to live as a whole person.

Daily she sought the Lord for wisdom, guidance and for grace to manage herself. She fed on the bread of the Word, rejoicing in her close walk with God.

Jeanie

Conclusion: Many times in this book, I will emphasize the importance of bonding. Severe consequences result in later life when this biological imperative of enmeshment with an empathic other, usually mother, is thwarted. The mirroring mother gives the child his sense of who he is and his unique value in the world. She also teaches him that life is an exciting adventure, despite the difficulties and hard work. By her reactions to events around her, she instructs the little one about reality. If she is frantic, emotionally overreacting to internal and external events, the baby becomes fearful. If mother calmly manages frustrations and disappointments, the child eagerly reaches out to learn about the world.

Unexpected severe emotional reactions, like Jeanie's, usually have their roots in the unconscious. The first job for a therapist in a crisis situation is alleviating the immediate danger. In Jeanie's case, if she had had to be hospitalized, Alison's bonding, through nursing, would have been severely disrupted. Offering nightly access is not possible in most cases. As I listen to the people sitting before me, I have to ascertain God's will. In Jeanie's case, I was perfectly sure God wanted me to extend myself. These are hard decisions, as every patient is infinitely important and I only have a limited amount of time. Pete and Jeanie were very grateful; their awareness led to intense efforts to maximize the benefits derived from our contacts.

In this case, I did a lot of psychological teaching. Understanding what's going on in the unconscious helps keep feelings in perspective during the therapy. As Jeanie battled daily with her anxious obsessions, she took comfort from knowledge of the process. Unrealistic expectations that Pete would make her feel better, as her mother had expected her father to make her feel better, melted away slowly as she came to understand God's plan for meeting her needs with Himself.

If Jeanie had not been filled with the Holy Spirit, the outlook would have been much less hopeful and therapy would have continued much longer. Working with the Holy Spirit in her allowed me to call Jeanie into a right relationship with God through Christ Jesus, as the disciples were called from their nets to rely exclusively on Him. We talked a lot during the months we were together about the commitment Jesus requires. He commands us to give up old ways, "Sell everything you have . . . to follow (Him)" (Mark 10:21). Only with radical obedience can we hope to get through the "eye of the needle" (Matthew 19:24).

The Hated Crib

Raising an infant also demands a radical commitment if that child is to grow up emotionally healthy. Only in Western culture do we allow mothers to separate infants from their bodies. In Africa, India, South America, and Asia, infants ride on the mother's back until well past two years of age. Our merchants like to sell cribs; our realtors like us to buy homes with extra bedrooms; our sex-obsessed society likes to encourage adults to consider their needs for comfort. Terrified babies scream for their mothers across America, while inexperienced young women are instructed by doctors and child-rearing manuals not to spoil their kids. The child becomes anxious, develops colic, has severe crying spells. The mother becomes frantic because she cannot comfort her baby, and the bonding is disrupted. War is declared.

Mother keeps trying to make baby be good and lie down in the crib to sleep; baby keeps trying to teach mother what he needs. Since he can't tell her in words, he shows her by refusing to settle down in the hated crib, or screaming in the middle of the night. A baby allowed to sleep with his mother in her bed until he is two years old, happily moves into his own bedroom. Only those children who, as infants, were terrified of being along in the dark, continue to cling to the mother or an object reminding them of the mother, such as a blanket or thumb, through the toddler years into school age.

Jeanie followed my advice. She carried her baby on her body during the day and slept with Alison at night. At two-and-a-half years of age, on my last checkup call, Alison is a calm little girl, sleeping in her own room. Her mother babysits two infants. Alison has adjusted very well to these little strangers on her mother's lap because she received enough attention in her first two years. A very good book on this subject is *The Continuum Concept* by Jean Liedloff. British researchers, Winnicott, Spitz, Mahler, Bowlby and Melanie Klein, also have addressed these issues at length.

De-glorifying Sex

Some therapists would have gone directly to work on the romantic and sexual difficulties in the marriage. I felt that would be raising false expectations in Jeanie that, somehow, Pete would compensate for her mother's deficits. Pete was very concerned about Jeanie's feelings and Alison's welfare, but he did not want to work on becoming more intimate. He felt "peopled out" by the end of the day. Pete could have been made to modify his behavior for awhile, I suppose, feigning interest in romantically approaching Jeanie, leading to sexual encounters. But it wouldn't have lasted, leaving each of them feeling like failures—she, for being unattractive (which she wasn't) and he, for not being a truly sexual man (which he was). Many men sublimate their sexual drive into their work, ambitiously pursuing goals and becoming very proficient in business.

The prevailing cultural notion, that everyone should want lots of sexual intercourse, fails to take into account that in most of the world sex is enjoyed but not glorified. Many married people go all their lives without much sexual activity with their mates. It is not the panacea for interpersonal happiness. If Pete and Jeanie both want to work on some aspects of their relationship in the future, that can be done; but my first concern was Jeanie's emotional stability so she could properly mother Alison. We achieved that goal.

"It is Christ that died, yea rather, that is risen again, who is even at the right hand of God, who also maketh intercession for us; the Spirit . . . maketh intercession for the saints according to the will of God" (Romans 8:34, 27 KJV).

2
Back Off Sexually

DAVID

Synopsis: David was a tall, handsome thirty-two-year-old insurance salesman, unable to make good money due to strong Christian beliefs about selling unneeded plans. He came to therapy complaining about a nonexistent sex life with his wife, Margie, age twenty-nine. This condition had prevailed since the birth of their second child, now eighteen months old. This obsession about his sexual deprivation consumed his thought life. He felt very angry.

Cognitive behavior modification coupled with new scripturally based insights about true holiness helped David put on the mind of Christ. His obedience allowed God to change the family dynamics and save his marriage.

Back Off Sexually

When David came to see me, he was very upset because his wife, Margie, wasn't eager to have sex any more. He said he was a very sexual man; every night he wanted to make love, but since the birth of their first child, she said she was too tired or had a headache. Margie was not eager to snuggle, much less have intercourse. He found himself obsessing about this all day long, wondering if he could persuade his wife to make love that night or being angry that he *had* to persuade.

David had been married to Margie for five years. They had a four-year-old boy and an eighteen-month-old girl. David and Margie met in a Christian organization and had gone together since the eleventh grade. She was the only girl he had ever dated seriously; he was her only boyfriend. Because they were very strong Christians reared in strict homes, they didn't go much further than kissing until they were married. Their church teachers had warned that fondling of breasts, French kissing or lying together, even if fully clothed, would put them on the slippery slide to perdition.

David had eagerly looked forward to their life together in marriage. The first year, while Margie wasn't exactly passionate, she was at least interested in trying to learn to become more spontaneous sexually. Then she suffered a difficult pregnancy; she was sick most of the time. David tried not to express his need more than once a week. She tolerated that much contact without enthusiasm. After the baby was born, he looked forward eagerly to resuming lovemaking. He dreamed of her really wanting him physically, reacting with intense pleasure to his ministrations.

This was not to be. After the birth of the child, she was so exhausted from caring for the infant that she accepted his advances most unwillingly. When the baby was a year old, David begged Margie to go with him to sexual counseling. She wasn't interested. She stated, "You have an unnatural need. Most men with small children recognize the pressure on their wives and don't insist on sexual contact."

A year later she got pregnant again. This time she totally shut him out. David was living a celibate life while married. He'd been taught that masturbation was sinful. He wasn't interested in committing adultery. He was stuck, and he resented it bitterly.

Childhood Yearnings

I asked David about his home life when he was a little boy. He'd been the middle child of five, with both an older and a younger sister and brother. His dad worked long hours as a hardware store owner to provide for his large family. They never lacked for any comforts. His mom helped his dad in the store, so the children often took care of themselves. David babysat his younger siblings and, by the time he was seven, was taking turns at preparing meals and doing the family laundry. Although there wasn't much money for vacations and lessons, there was plenty of activity around his house with so many children close in age. He and his brothers did a lot of fighting, physically and verbally. "Anything you can do I can do better" was their motto.

David did well academically and was an outstanding tennis player. He never got involved in team sports because he was shy and didn't like all the hours of group drills. He enjoyed practicing his tennis for several hours a day and then would go home to read or listen to his stereo. For a little while David thought he would be a writer; he wrote some poems and started a novel.

He got along with his schoolmates, but never really felt he was part of the gang. He did not have any really close friends. The family members had each other and didn't need to gather any more kids to play tennis or talk. In high school he felt unsure of himself around girls. When Margie sought him out at a Christian young people's meeting, he was flattered. David enjoyed her and never looked for another woman. He was with her whenever he could arrange it. He carried her around in his mind and mentally talked to her.

David said he fantasized a lot after he met Margie while he was off doing his stint in the army. He imagined them as one flesh. He dreamed about their being together and enjoying each other in every way. It seemed as if his lifelong sense of isolation would be over when he got married.

As soon as he was discharged from the army, they were married. He took a job as an insurance salesman with a Christian company. He had always been very adept with numbers and easily learned all the plans. The only problem was that he wasn't a very aggressive salesman. When a family clearly didn't need one of his products, he discouraged their spending money uselessly. Despite working diligently, he never made a good income.

David told me that Margie was very musical. By the time she was nine, she was playing the piano for some of the services at the family's church and she sang solos in a sweet voice. At school she was shy and without self-confidence. She was very pretty with long brown hair and brown eyes set in a charming face.

Margie was the oldest of two girls. Her younger sister, Holly, was outgoing and exuberant. Her dad was a lawyer specializing in probate; her mom stayed home. She was a perfectionist, methodical about getting the household chores done, and somewhat humorless. David said Margie's mother was always very kind and thoughtful but he didn't think she got much fun out of life.

David never saw any signs of affection between Margie's mom and dad. They were courteous and appropriate but there wasn't any spark jumping between them. Margie's dad had published a number of articles and tended to spend time, when he wasn't reading or preparing cases, writing in his study. Margie said he looked ridiculous when he tried to get on the children's level to play a game. She and her sister were usually relieved when he retreated to his study.

The three women got along very well together, almost like triplets. Holly had not married as yet. She was off in Japan working as an office manager in one of the American Express offices and touring on weekends with a variety of young men, all of whom seemed to be rather footloose and fancy-free. Holly's absence made Margie's mom ever more dependent on Margie, and the two women talked daily by phone. David and Margie went over every Sunday afternoon with the children to his in-laws' house for dinner.

I asked David about their relationships with God. David assured me that they were very devout Christians. They read the Scripture together daily, went to church twice on Sundays and on Wednesday nights were in a small kinship group. They participated in the administration tasks of the church as well as in the spiritual leadership. Both of them were trained Bible teachers; they thoroughly enjoyed exegeting Scripture.

David reported that he had been brought up in the Episcopal church. When he was sixteen he met the Lord in a new and powerful way, receiving the baptism of the Holy Spirit while on a weekend retreat. His passionate devotion to Jesus was a hindrance in making money, as the business world seemed to be full of double-dealing and forked-tongue talking.

Margie was also born again when she was in high school at a revival meeting that had come to her church. She sought God's will earnestly, praying daily for others.

A Significant Other

I learned all this in our first hour together. David wanted help with his sexual problems. These are some of the thoughts that were going through my head as I listened to David talk. In my mind's eye, I saw this tall, gangly, shy, ruggedly handsome young man growing up in the midst of a busy family, lonely for special attention and love. I could picture David yearning from his earliest days for one special person, a significant other, who would know and cherish him, filling his chronic emptiness. Their union would be physical, emotional and spiritual, joining them together as one flesh. I'm sure he always imagined his woman would yearn for him with the same deep need that he experienced.

Despite having two sisters, David knew nothing about the difference between men's and women's sexual needs. Perhaps his sisters didn't know either. I doubt if their mom or dad chose to discuss how frustrating it is for most young men to have to deal with the fact that many young women are not terribly interested in sex. Women are much more interested in sex in their early thirties as their biological clocks push them to have children. By then, men's burning needs have often tapered off.

David felt that he was being personally rejected because his beloved was not eager for sex any more. He didn't have many friends with whom he could discuss these matters; he wasn't the kind of guy to sit around and shoot the breeze. In the army, he'd spent much of his spare time reading or playing tennis rather than downing beers with the boys while swapping girl stories. David was longing for a lady with whom he could become enmeshed.

Best Friends

Margie grew up as a shy, musical little girl without much frustration because she never had to individuate from her mother and sister. She was, and still is, enmeshed with both of them. When her normal developmental individuation periods came at two, six, thirteen, and eighteen years of age, her mother made it so comfortable to remain best friends that Margie never got loose. This happens in many families, particularly religious families. Pastors often perceive developmentally appropriate distancing by a youngster from his family as dangerous to his spiritual welfare. They encourage staying together.

Probably, Margie's mom and dad weren't available for each other. Her dad gained his sense of fulfillment from his work and his writing; her mother relied on the girls and her home. It's not at all difficult to understand how Margie's mom found it easy to meet the needs of her shy, oldest daughter. They shopped, talked, ate, played games, laughed, and went bicycling together throughout Margie's childhood. Her mom was a quiet, giving lady who gained great joy being empathic with her daughters and supporting them in any way she could. Margie never learned what men needed, nor did she learn to give in order to receive. Her mother gave naturally; Margie took naturally, as an infant takes. I'm sure Margie accepted the Lord as comfortably and easily as she accepted her mother's unconditional love. When she did make contact with her dad, it was a pleasant, formal interchange, mirroring her comfortable relationship with the living God.

I hypothesize that Margie expected David to be just like her mother, warm, cheerful, and supportive. It never occurred to her that he would ask when she wasn't in the mood for giving, that he would need when she didn't need, or that he would expect her to do what she didn't feel in the mood for doing.

It's Like Getting in Bed with a Bicycle

The first year of their marriage was comfortable and easy. She didn't much like sex but she did want a child and it was sort of an interesting new game to play. When she became pregnant, it was another ball game. She was nauseated for the first six months; it was all she could do just to get the housework finished. The thought of having to have sexual intercourse was not pleasant.

She really felt demeaned and was uncomfortable with David's demands; she could easily live without any sexual activity. It surprised her that David wasn't equally as comfortable with celibacy.

I had asked David what making love to Margie was like when she did acquiesce to his request. He said, "It is like getting in bed with a bicycle. She doesn't move; she doesn't respond. She just lies there letting me caress and kiss her. I have never been able to turn her on. I try to talk to her while making love, but her mind doesn't seem to be in the room. She won't tell me what she is thinking." He paused a moment and then added, bitterly, "I doubt if it is about making love to me."

My guess is that Margie really didn't have any interest in becoming sexually turned on or orgasmic. I believe her mother sublimated her sexuality into childcare so Margie didn't have a model. Tired from her new infant, Margie had even less interest in contact with David's body. She really wished she could go home and have her mother give her some relief from the twenty-four-hour daily care required by the little one. She wasn't used to supporting her own emotional and physical needs much less being available to her son and husband on a full-time basis. The glamour of being married wore off rapidly and Margie became resentful and withdrawn.

Don't Ask for Sex Anymore

Given these speculations, what to do? I could ask David to bring Margie in and say to her that her husband needed sex. She might agree to give it to him once a week, maybe even twice a week, which she would probably do reluctantly for a few months. However, I doubted I could quicken her enthusiasm for her husband's body by executive decree.

I could have sent them to a sex therapist, but Margie had already said she had no interest in that kind of exploration. I could diagnose the games they were playing using the Transactional Analysis model or explain the dynamic problems which gave them an unrealistic expectation of marriage. Head knowledge might be interesting but it wouldn't solve David's problem. Somehow I had to change the family system or the marriage would not last much longer.

I said to David, "Don't ask your wife for sex anymore."

He was appalled. "How in the world can a Christian psychologist suggest that a man not have access to his wife's body? Saint Paul made it perfectly clear that it is a husband's right to enjoy marital union."

"I know the Scriptures," I answered. "But if you want your marriage to last, you're going to have to withdraw your nightly requests. Furthermore, I want to see you in therapy every week for six months to help you not need a woman."

We talked about the various people in the Bible who learned to stand alone. David's yearning for a soul mate, a significant other, had begun when he was a very tiny boy, but it was not a realistic expectation. It came from his longing for his mama who was caring for his younger brother and sister. He felt lonely and unwanted.

I told him that the yearning was for God; his soul could only be satisfied by God. Margie could be his covenanted helpmate. They would raise the children and witness to the world that a Christian marriage is blessed but she could not be the yearned-for beloved. It simply wasn't part of God's game plan.

God tells us in several places in the Bible that He is jealous. He wants to be the intimate, the significant other, for us. If He allowed us to keep intense relationships on earth, we would never seek for Him. We would become complacent; our spiritual growth would stop. He allows deep passions during our lives for brief periods so we can experience that kind of love, as a foretaste of the union He wants with us. Love on this earth, most of the time, as Jesus taught us, should be agape love—love without need.

A Wife's Fury

When David told Margie he wasn't going to ask for sex again, she was furious. She said he'd consulted a stupid psychologist. We are often called all manner of names. Ah well, Scripture says "Rejoice!" "Blessed are you when people insult you, persecute you and falsely say all kinds of evil against you because of me. Rejoice and be glad" (Matthew 5:11). She sulked around the house for three days and would not talk to him. David called me the second night. He was beginning to lose confidence in our plan. I could really empathize with his state of mind. However, I said, "Be of good cheer and hold tight." So he did. I held the family in my prayers.

David came to see me two weeks later. He said he couldn't believe how pleasant life was around his house.

Startled, I asked, "Really? What's changed?"

"I don't know. Maybe it's something about the atmosphere. We're doing a lot more laughing. Even the children seem to sense that something is different."

"Are you acting differently toward Margie, or she toward you?"

"I don't think I am acting any differently toward her." He paused. "Maybe I've lightened up a little now that I have firmly given up any hope of having sex. But Margie is very different. She seems to be much more open and responsive toward me. She acts eager to see me when I get home and is interested in listening to my day's adventures. She has even moved over toward me in bed several times to snuggle. She's never done that before." I was thrilled.

Programming Dreams

I told David, "Anything can be communicated to Junior (his unconscious) every night just before you fall asleep by intensely picturing it. Junior David is about two years old; he doesn't understand words very well. Therefore, every night, just before you go to sleep, program your 'REM' sleep with mental pictures. (Rapid Eye Movement sleep refers to the two hours of dreaming that we all do every night divided into seven segments.) The clear picture to transmit is of your intimate connection to God. See Him in clear images enjoying you as you enjoy Him. It will take Junior six weeks to get the message, but then your frantic, internal yearning will cease. Obsessions come from our unconscious."

It's perfectly clear that David was skeptical about my understanding of human behavior but he bravely decided to give it a try. Every night he saw himself walking and talking with God on high mountain passes. He heard the words they spoke. David knew the restlessness of his soul would only find rest in God, as Saint Augustine puts it.

Two months later David remarked, "Something weird is happening. I must be losing my libidinal drive."

"Oh, really?"

"Yeah, I don't have the great yearning to make love that I've experienced since I was fifteen years old."

"Is there any chance that Junior has changed his mind and is now expecting a different kind of fulfillment?"

"Well," he replied, "I guess it has been a little more than six weeks since I started programming my REM sleep. But I don't want to stop being a man."

I assured him, "Not much chance, buddy. That's the least of our worries. You're sublimating your sexuality as did many of the men in the Bible. Creativity is a higher use of the sex drive than intercourse. Only adolescents believe erections equate with masculinity. How's it going at home?"

"Fine. I can't believe how fine. We are getting along better than we ever have since our marriage. My wife now wants to snuggle every night, which I love; we fall asleep in each other's arms. It is much easier for us to talk and play together."

"What do you mean to play together?"

"I don't know, exactly. We are silly together. Life doesn't feel so serious at home. I really enjoy coming home now because we banter and play silly jokes on the kids and each other."

A Surprising Seduction

A month later David came in looking very sheepish.

He said, "I blew it."

"You did what? Are you telling me that after three months you asked your wife for intercourse?"

"No, no," he exclaimed. "I didn't ask my wife. She asked me and I refused."

"Good, that's terrific. What do you mean you blew it?"

"Well, she begged and begged and then she got in bed and snuggled. She rubbed my back and my arms and my legs and I lost it. I gave in."

I asked, "You gave in? You allowed your wife to seduce you?"

"Yes, and I'm really very embarrassed! I almost didn't come in to see you today because I thought you'd probably give me a bad time."

"How did it go? Was it fun?"

He grinned, "It was wonderful. It was really wonderful; I had no idea that she could get that turned on."

"Really? What happened?"

"Well," he said, "I was lying there trying to remember how I was supposed to avoid giving in to her blandishments. She was using every trick in the book to get me turned on. Finally, I couldn't control myself any longer; she was delighted to see that she was affecting my body; it turned her on in a way that had never happened before. Anyway, one thing led to another. I really resisted which only excited her more. Finally she got on top of me and we took off. She had the first orgasm of her life that night."

"That night? Do you mean to tell me this has happened more than once since I saw you last?" I asked, looking sternly at David.

He looked rueful. "Well, I've stuck to my promise. I've never initiated it. But she's initiated two other times. She's gotten on top of me and become very excited. Today she called me at work and said 'I can't wait until you get home 'cause I want to touch,' which is our word for making love." David looked chagrined like a naughty boy.

"How did you feel?"

"I felt really wonderful. My wife isn't frigid. She really isn't frigid. As long as I don't push or scare her, I think she's going to get more and more in touch with her own sexuality. I'm so excited for her." Then David asked, "Okay, Doc? I mean the way we're doing it now; is it okay?"

Enthusiastically, I replied, "Sure, it's wonderful, a true miracle of the Lord's. You were willing to discipline yourself, as have all the saints of old, and He's rewarding you with a wife who wants to learn how to make wonderful love to you. As the Bible says,

'Rejoice in the Lord always; I will say it again: Rejoice!' (Philippians 4:4). Our God can be trusted when we leave everything in His hands, counting on Him to teach us through adversity the desires that are not appropriate, and make miracles occur when we are obedient."

David and Margie went on to become extremely close physically, emotionally, and spiritually. Last time I saw them, four years after I had worked with David, they were the very model of a loving, Christian family. The kids were terrific, bright, healthy, and joyful. Praise God!

Expectations

Conclusion: Obsessions are defenses against uncomfortable or unacceptable unconscious material. David, as a small child, felt unloved and was angry at his family for ignoring him. Little boys do not dare to feel their murderous rage toward those who feed, house, clothe, and emotionally nourish them, even if all they get are crumbs. So they repress feelings, often growing up shy and self-conscious, never really being able to relax around people. David's repressed material reappeared in adult sexual terms as a hopeless yearning for closeness with Margie alternating with intense anger at needing to beg for sexual intimacy.

Even if I could somehow have increased Margie's appetite for intercourse, it would not have satisfied David. Unconsciously there could never be enough loving, because his mother wasn't able to meet his needs when he was an infant. When he reached for his father at the developmentally appropriate age of three, he was preoccupied with trying to earn money. David grew up believing God had put a woman on earth just for him who would be his soul mate, the perfect other to mirror his wants and needs. These expectations, encouraged by his pastor, made the task of individuation from his enmeshment with the idealized Margie in his head, very difficult. Of course, there would be moments when Margie would satisfy and comfort David, as she did when she reached for him sexually or they did silly things with their kids, but he had to be weaned from his expectations.

It was important to understand Margie's attitudes toward sex as well, because her mother's modeling of grownup attitudes and behaviors profoundly affected the little girls. As Margie grew up she learned that the highest form of love was *philia*—sisterly love—because her mother preferred the company of the girls over her husband. Following her mother's example, Margie only wanted babies and support from David. Without her gaining insight into this early training, it would have been difficult to quicken her sexuality.

Cognitive behavior modification was the primary treatment of choice, followed by analysis of David's unconscious motivations. His frame of reference had to be changed. That was not very difficult because he knew the people in the Bible and was Spirit-filled. For insights into self-supported living, we could scrutinize Jesus, who was unmarried, or Peter, who left his wife for long periods, or Paul, who suggests celibacy as the highest calling. Despite the prevailing cultural norms, sexual singleness can be blessed within or outside of marriage.

David rapidly altered his habitual way of being in the world once he understood because the Holy Spirit indwelt in him. God performs miracles regularly for those who are obedient—in fact, He makes them sons and daughters (John 1:12).

Neither of us knew what would happen when David stopped approaching Margie for sex. He was not being abstinent as a paradoxical intention. (That means saying or doing something exactly the opposite from what you really want, to make the other person change his position.) David was obedient to God's plan discerned as we spoke during the session. If David had hopes Margie would respond by becoming interested in genital contact, he would have been manipulating her rather than obeying God. I warned him to say firmly, "Get thee behind me, Satan" (Matthew 16:23 KJV), if such thoughts strayed into his mind. He gave up his cherished sexual obsessions despite his doubts and the Lord "credited it to him as righteousness" (Genesis 15:6).

Because "the old man" continues to dwell in us even while we are being transformed into the image and likeness of Christ (2

Corinthians 3:18), David could easily have begun to take Margie's new interest in him as the way things would be in the future. Counting on God's gifts rather than His all-sufficient grace plays directly into the Devil's hands. Expecting Margie to want him even one night would shift the miracle into an expectation: "It's about time Margie grew up and began acting like a proper Christian wife!" We take God's daily miracles of health and food and love for granted. We whine whenever we don't get our wishes, forgetting it was because of obedience to God's way that Abraham was called "friend" (James 2:23).

Analysis of David's unconscious thoughts, feelings and perceptions allowed him to become aware of his defenses against the conflicts raging below the repression barrier. Once he had insight, David could consciously disengage from immature attitudes and feelings formed when he was a needy child. Now he realized he wasn't helpless anymore, as he had been when longing for his distracted mother. He could mother his Junior; in fact, he was the very best possible caretaker for the little one inside because he was always with him, as a good mother is always with her infant.

Analysis also allowed him to replace less efficient defenses like obsessing, intellectualizing, and rationalizing with the highest level defenses. Humor, anticipation, altruism, sublimation, and suppression became consciously chosen ways of handling stressful situations. David engaged in strenuous exercise (sublimation), forced his mind to memorize Psalms whenever old thought patterns began (suppression), and through anticipation avoided advice giving or receiving, stressful situations such as arguments, and psychobabble (unnecessarily technical psychological jargon which tends to obscure rather than clarify what's really taking place). He invested himself in the youth ministry at the church (altruism) and practiced seeing the comic side of everything (humor). Every night as he went to sleep, David thanked God for his progress, knowing it was possible only because of the indwelling Holy Spirit; he forgave himself any lapses, forgave others, and recommitted his heart, soul, mind and strength to seeking the kingdom of God. (Matthew 6:33; 22:37).

Seeking Wisdom

In psychological terms, David began to seek the maturity and wisdom found in the outstanding men and women of many centuries and cultures. They have a calmness, a lack of urgency, a twinkle in the eye, and an ability to see the glass half-full rather than half-empty. They enjoy small, everyday things and are content in all situations (Philippians 4:11). They are nondefensive, open to new experiences, good listeners, quick to forgive and accept forgiveness, thankful and in touch with a higher power. They look at life and death with equanimity—not clutching for power, wealth, and respect, or fearing not having or being. They are not anxious for tomorrow, because nothing really matters except their relationship with the living God however they conceptualize Him. They are not boastful or vain; the other's welfare is their primary concern.

On the American Indian wheel of life, the highest occupation is to be one of those who defend the rights of children. They are called gamblers because every morning their prayer is "If I fail to protect the children, this is a good day to die." By children, they mean all the helpless, poor, needy, sick, imprisoned, and weary people in the world.

David grew, and as he grew, Margie became much more cognizant of a life beyond dedication just to her house and children. They are firmly on the way to becoming enlightened saints.

"The Lord . . . has sent me, that thou mightest receive thy sight, and be filled with the Holy Ghost" (Acts 9:17 KJV).

3

You Have a Right to Harmony

MARCIE

S*ynopsis:* An attractive, well-groomed, twenty-nine-year-old mother came to get help handling her difficult son. At seven, Jason was a terror at school and at home, in danger of flunking second grade. The older sister was easy to manage; but Marcie and her husband, Jim, lost control around Jason, resulting in daily yelling. A solid transference relationship, coupled with Marcie's desperation, allowed us to change the family systems. Marcie trusted me enough to share her inappropriate actions and reactions. Insights led to new ways of being with the children. As the identified problem, Jason's behavior was self-reinforcing. He carried the family's badness. Careful analysis revealed Marcie's strong need to recreate her chaotic original family. Jim was unable to stabilize Jason due to his own fatherless home background and alcoholic mother. Though incomplete because Jim feared psychological exploration, the therapy settled Marcie, allowing Jason to quiet down and become academically superior.

You Have a Right to Harmony

Marcie came to me because she was having difficulty handling her seven-year-old son. He was a very bright, almost hyperactive child, always taking things apart, arguing, moving around. The school had called and said that unless she got some psychological help for Jason, they were afraid he would not be able to complete second grade. In class he pestered the other children, couldn't stay in his seat, had a short attention span, and was unable to complete assignments. He was intelligent and fully aware of the work that had to be done, but he couldn't settle himself for very long to accomplish a task. Marcie had tried a variety of behavior-modification schemes at home, such as insisting that he do his homework before watching television, time out, or grounding him. None of them seemed to work. He continued to be disruptive, not only in the classroom, but also at home, carrying on a continual verbal sparring match with either his mother, father, or older sister.

His sister did very well in school. Heather was three years older than Jason. She went quietly about her own business. Marcie ruefully remembered her superior attitude toward parents of children in Heather's class who were having difficulty getting their children to settle down in school. Heather had been so easy that it was hard for her to understand why Jason was so difficult. She didn't think anything had changed in her mothering style or in her relationship with her husband.

Several friends had told her that Jason was hyperactive but the pediatrician had not confirmed that diagnosis, nor was she willing to put Jason on medication. Jason was in a church school, following family tradition. She wanted him to receive religious training even though she knew some teachers were underqualified and classes were too large. They didn't have the knowledge or resources to help Jason.

Marcie's way of handling Jason's defiance and disobedience was to yell. Every time she yelled, Jim would get into the act and start yelling too, both at Jason and at Marcie. Heather would lock herself in her room. Marcie had come from an argumentative family. She hated her mom and dad's daily quarrels. Now she was horrified by the damage this arguing was doing to her own children. With Jason around, life felt very much out of control. When he was at school or staying overnight with his grandmother, everything settled down. She, Jim and Heather had a cheerful, quiet time together. As soon as Jason came into the house, havoc ensued.

Why Was Everybody Else So Good?

I was trying to sort out why Jason was so bad and everybody else so good. I am fully aware that some children are very difficult. The question was whether the family was getting anything out of encouraging Jason to behave badly. In some families, one person is considered difficult so everybody else can feel good about themselves. They are relieved from having to own their own less than desirable qualities. The identified person carries the burden of the family's negative feelings and angry moods. Was Jason a difficult child or did the family need a scapegoat?

What made Marcie lose control of the situation? She was a very attractive young woman, conservatively dressed, well-groomed, active in the community. She seemed to be very insightful and competent in a number of different areas. How could one small boy render her so powerless?

How did Jim play into this scenario? Why did he allow a small seven-year-old boy to disrupt the household? What internal dynamics kept him from taking charge and insisting that Jason stop it?

I asked Marcie about Jim's background. She said that he had grown up as an only child, raised by an alcoholic mother who started drinking after the death of her husband before Jim was born. Jim frequently had to pull her out of bars in Los Angeles, take her home and put her to bed.

He became a good basketball player. Every afternoon after school, he practiced until dark and in high school was the star of the team. He won a basketball scholarship to a prestigious western college. Jim was one of the hardest working, most dedicated players on the team.

After college he became a real estate salesman and put as much energy into selling commercial real estate as he had into basketball. He was always talking about get-rich-quick schemes, studying money magazines and looking for special deals. He gambled with their money often on various hot deals. Sometimes they made money and sometimes they lost.

Jim had Jason's physical restlessness; he had difficulty sitting still to watch television or read a novel. He slept so soundly he never heard the babies cry. Every morning, bright and early, Jim would run seven miles before going to work.

I asked Marcie about her childhood. She had grown up in a Czechoslovakian family where everybody let their feelings hang out. Whatever you felt, you made sure everybody else in the room, or in the house—or in the neighborhood—heard about it. Not only her parents, but all her aunts, uncles, and cousins thought family occasions meant drinking a lot and loudly sharing opinions. They would fight about anything: politics, religion, the weather, baseball games, the children, the state of the economy—anything. An early memory was of sitting at a Christmas dinner listening to the relatives quarreling, pounding on the table, as they poured drinks.

I asked Marcie if Jim was alcoholic.

She said, "Heavens, no! He just drinks white wine."

"How much?"

"Oh, I don't know but it's not real drinking. I come from a family of real drinkers and he just consumes white wine."

I asked her if she drank.

"No, never! I saw enough of its effect as a child. I don't like the taste or how it makes me feel."

A Whole New Way of Being

I told Marcie, "You could choose to have harmony around you, insisting that people not disturb your space. You can require that, at least where you are, people behave in a calm, courteous, cheerful manner." Marcie looked at me with absolute astonishment. It had never occurred to her. Her life as a youngster had felt so chaotic emotionally that the thought that calmness was a natural right took her by surprise.

"Doctor, I'd like that. I'd like to be able to live in a calm space."

"Good. To achieve that goal, which will also help Jason get control of himself, you'll need to come see me once a week for awhile."

Marcie agreed readily. "All right. I'd be happy to do that. I know I have to learn a whole new way of being in the world."

What Marcie had to learn was harmony. In Japan, it is called "wa." In the old days a nobleman was served by fierce warriors called Samurai. They were responsible for seeing that their nobleman's *wa* was not disturbed. If, intentionally or by accident, a Samurai disturbed his nobleman's *wa*, the nobleman could order him to disembowel himself—commit Hari Kari. The harmony of nature is so precious to the Japanese that they build exquisite gardens and rake gravel to resemble the waves of the ocean. They quiet themselves by contemplating these arrangements. The Japanese warriors of the noble class were trained to perform all the intricate, dancelike motions of the tea ceremony. Christians know about the necessity for *wa* because we have been ordered to "be still, and know that I am God" (Psalm 46:10).

In medieval times anybody who was rich enough went on retreats to monasteries as often as possible for the stillness. They removed themselves from the hustle and bustle of daily living to search for God through the quieting of their minds and bodies. Nowadays, recreation means running through twelve countries in sixteen days or partying to loud music. Stillness, harmony, and pleasure in one's own company have almost vanished in twentieth century America.

Marcie turned out to be a willing learner. She always came to her therapy sessions on time and brought the material of her daily life, as well as her dreams. We learned about the little girl inside her—Junior Marcie. Junior's strong opinions about the nature of reality controlled Marcie's behavior. Unfortunately, Junior was formed when Marcie was very young so her understanding of how things worked was inaccurate. Her perceptions dominated Marcie's experiencing of the world despite the subsequent thirty years of learning.

The Freudians call Junior the unconscious and/or pre-conscious. Carl Rogers calls Junior the actual child submerged under the adaptive child we all become, conforming to social expectations. Many personality theorists have some kind of a label for this strong-minded, willful infant buried in each of us. They differ as to how much influence the little one has on our adult behavior.

Some feel, as does Albert Ellis, the founder of Rational-Emotive psychotherapy, that if you can just explain to somebody rationally that they shouldn't be yelling, they can stop. In my experience that's true if the two-year-old is not addicted to "uproar," to use Berne's Transactional Analysis term. Addiction to "uproar" is like addiction to anything else. A person becomes anxious and jittery without it. Dr. Ellis might have said, "Marcie, stop fighting. Stop letting Jason distress your household." But I knew she had been told that by many people before. She had tried to quiet things down. She was devastated that her house was so chaotic.

My guess was that those patterns were deeply buried in Marcie's psyche; she couldn't just choose to stop. She needed to learn to inhibit her first impulse when something went wrong and inhibit her words when Jason teased her. Those conscious inhibitions of unconscious reactions would allow her time to react more appropriately. The harmony she fervently desired could become a reality.

I Can Have Harmony

Week by week, as our relationship grew stronger, Marcie began to find herself mentally consulting me before she did or said anything. In difficult situations, she would literally think, *What would Georgie say in this situation? How would Georgie tell me to handle myself?* Those thoughts gave her just enough time to choose an appropriate course of action.

For example, when Jason came home from school, threw his books down in the living room, spilled his milk, yelled at his sister and told his mother that she was really stupid because she gave him the wrong kind of lunch that day, Marcie would carefully control her reactions. When Jim came home, frantic because one of his get-rich-quick schemes had not materialized, or when he began pointing out to her that she wasn't managing the household very well, or that she didn't really love him, Marcie could think before speaking.

As we talked to Junior Marcie through dreams, we helped the little one grow up and see that her beliefs about the truth of life were not accurate. Junior actively entered into our correction of her perceptions and opinions. Week by week, through Marcie's dreams, she informed us of her maturing frame of reference.

Each session Marcie would state emphatically at least once, "I can have harmony around me! I have a right to peace and courtesy in my daily life!"

"That's true. God does not intend for us to live in a chaotic environment," I agreed.

"I don't want the children to grow up in a chaotic, strife-torn home. I'm afraid, when they have families, patterns will repeat themselves."

I assured her, "By changing your ways now, the 'sin of the fathers' will not go down 'to the third and fourth generation'" (Exodus 20:5).

As Marcie continued in therapy, she learned basic ways of working with the children. She learned never to criticize the children and seldom give advice. Instead she asked questions so the children could draw appropriate conclusions. If she wanted Jason or Heather to do anything on a regular basis, those chores were posted on the refrigerator near a box of gold stars so they could put them in the appropriate square as they completed each task. At the end of the week a dime was paid for each star. If she wanted something done that was not on the chart, Marcie would write a note and give the children twenty-four hours to accomplish the task.

The Vacuum Cleaner Monster

I told her about the vacuum cleaner monster who came every Monday morning to my house to pick up everything that was out of place in the children's rooms. When she first told Jason about the vacuum cleaner monster, he laughed a lot and said she made it up. She replied she had heard that it was coming on Monday morning so she just wanted to be sure he knew. Monday morning came and Jason's room was a mess. Marcie went into it and put everything out of place in big garbage bags. A neighbor stored them in her garage. When Jason came home that afternoon from school, most of the things he played with were gone. Angrily he said, "Where are my toys?"

Marcie sighed, "Oh dear, I was afraid it was the vacuum cleaner monster."

"What do you mean?"

"I heard a clankity-bang, clankity-bang, clankity-bang and then a slurping sound. I was afraid that the vacuum cleaner monster had come."

Jason exclaimed, "What nonsense! There is no such thing as a vacuum cleaner monster. Give me back my toys!"

"They must be in the vacuum cleaner monster's tummy. I heard he collects toys for the poor children, so maybe he slurps them up and then vomits them out at the Salvation Army."

Jason yelled, "Stop that stupid talk! I want my toys back right now!"

Calmly, "I don't know where the monster lives."

"You're lying to me, Mother. You know perfectly well you took my toys. Give them back to me this minute!"

Quietly, "Are you calling me a liar, son? Are you questioning my word?" She refused to discuss it further. She suggested an alternative explanation. Marcie did not like to lie to Jason. She was careful not to get caught in an argument using the monster story to avoid having to insist once again on a clean room.

The next Sunday Marcie reminded Jason that the vacuum cleaner monster might come again. He scoffed loudly, saying that the vacuum cleaner monster was none other than his mother. She said, "Whatever." The next Monday morning after Jason had gone to school, she went into his room. To her delight, it was neat. She didn't dare look into the drawers to see where things had been stuffed, but it was picked up and tidy. She went to the neighbor, took back her garbage bag full of toys and placed them on the floor in Jason's room. When Jason came home that day, he asked, "Where did my toys come from?"

"Oh my, the vacuum cleaner monster must have reappeared. That's what I thought when I heard a clankity-bang, clankity-bang, clankity-bang this morning just after you left for school."

"Oh Mother," Jason was exasperated, "cut out that nonsense!"

"Nonsense? Where did your toys come from? Maybe the vacuum cleaner monster vomited them back out on your rug."

"That's gross, Mother!"

The next Monday morning all the toys in his room were put away. Marcie never had to discuss room cleaning with Jason again. On my advice, she kept the door to his room closed during the week, thereby avoiding the trauma of being distressed at the mess in a normal boy's room. But Monday mornings it was always in order.

Jim took Jason to the toy store every weekend. He paid him dimes, carefully counted out from a roll Jim had picked up from the bank, for each of the stars on the chart. They spent an hour Friday afternoon, or Saturday morning, walking through the store studying options, discussing pros and cons. Jim had a real chance to understand how Jason thought by watching his reasoning process around purchasing. They discussed the merits of delayed gratification, saving up money for several weeks to obtain a more expensive toy versus buying something less valuable immediately.

They analyzed the merits of various types of toys, noting how well each item was made, speculating whether it would last for awhile or break almost immediately. Jim allowed Jason to make his own mistakes. He purchased toys that didn't last until sundown and learned to be careful. He purchased on impulse and had to put off getting toys he really wanted. The "men" had an activity that they did habitually, about which they could talk during the week.

Heather insisted, of course, on having a chart, too. It was clear to her that this was a good way to make money. Her chart had little squares for each day and all of the expected activities were listed. Brushing her teeth, making the bed, getting appropriately dressed for school, making her lunch, feeding the dog, doing the dishes after supper—all the habitual daily and weekly chores that she performed were on the chart. She put gold stars in the designated squares. Being three years older, Heather often saved her money for special clothes, as she had outgrown many toys.

Marcie decided not to buy toys for the children, and on birthdays and Christmas, to start giving them modest presents. Jason and Heather had been overindulged for years. Their rooms were stuffed with all kinds of elaborate, often barely used items. Marcie started to only buy needed clothes for Heather. Extra shoes, sweaters, or jewelry were withheld so she would have an incentive to earn her own money. I knew that it was crucial that by the time Heather was a teenager she have some idea of the value and durability of clothes.

Turning Off the Tube

The third thing Marcie did was to take one of the main tubes out of the television. She didn't know what would happen. As with most American families, the children watched two to three hours of television every day, as did the parents. I urged her to discover the pleasures of conversation and of making popcorn. Marcie waited for the outraged screams. Sure enough, all of her family members objected violently for the first three days. Then they settled down and began to talk to each other, to play games, to take walks in the evening. Marcie and Heather did some creative cooking.

Marcie taught her family not to react to Jason's teasing. Slowly the behavior phased out. Without reinforcement any behavior in a normal person will become extinguished. In two months, Jason had stopped being belligerent. I don't want to give the impression that he became a calm, quiet, easy-to-get-along-with youngster. That's not true. But he did learn to manage himself; the "uproar" he was playing stopped getting the desired results. If Jason said something deliberately provocative, everybody ignored him and went on with what they were doing. When he knocked over the milk intentionally or slammed the door, he was sent to his room to cool off because he was disturbing the harmony of the family.

Marcie took to that concept like a duck to water. She no longer would serve on committees where acrimony or gossip were the order of the day. She could smile sweetly at Jim when he began to shout, and say, "My blood pressure is rising, dear; I think I'll take a short walk," rather than enter into a heated debate. Whenever anyone was angry, Marcie would hold up their jogging shoes and suggest they take a fast run around the block. She was more than willing to discuss any problems, but not in an atmosphere of tension and recriminations.

The Miracle Continues

Six years later, I am happy to report, Marcie is still prioritizing her harmony. Jason is on the honor roll in junior high school and Heather is a cheerleader with a straight-A average. In their home quiet is the order of the day. Jason has a much longer attention span and can sit quietly while doing a task. He's not angelic like Heather, but he is fitting in socially and enjoying his friends.

The therapeutic miracle happened when Marcie realized she had a right to demand harmony from others to maintain her inner peace. She worked for eight months, intensively, in therapy, straightening out some of Junior Marcie's misperceptions by routinely examining her habitual reactions. I tried to persuade Jim to come in for some therapy. I knew how severely damaged his unconscious was from the perceived abandonment by his father before he was born leaving him with an alcoholic mother. Jim would have none of it. He came to talk to me a couple of times about his wife and his children, but as far as examining his own life, or discussing different ways he might respond to situations, he wasn't interested. However, he was more than willing to follow Marcie's lead in terms of managing the children and was very pleased by her increasing centeredness.

Marcie's walk with the Lord grew deeper every day. She had been a good Baptist when I met her, but had not had time due to the uproar in her environment to spend meaningful time with Jesus. As the family settled down, she found herself joyfully praying all day long, practicing the presence of God while going about her daily rounds.

Marcie

Conclusions: Many clients do not have an internal picture of mature adult behavior. Raised by immature parents, they fall into repetition of the original atmosphere, often forcing a child or mate to provoke them. Marcie examined faulty family systems contributing to Jason's bad behavior. She learned to recognize her own inappropriate actions and verbalizations, as well as her husband's immaturity and potential substance abuse. Beer and wine are the leading beverages consumed by alcoholics. Children of alcoholics are at a very high risk of becoming addicted.

Even though unable to work with Jim, Marcie and I were able to reorganize the way the family related. Clean boundaries, separation for disturbing behavior, a ban on TV (which encourages hyperactivity and violence), rewards for consistent good behavior (gold stars), consequences with humor (vacuum cleaner monster), and a policy not to advise or criticize—all these steps made for a much more harmonious atmosphere.

The HAASS Defense

Marcie was delighted to learn she had a right to keep control of the space around her, requiring the family to stay peaceful and centered. She solved her unconscious conflicts between need for connectedness and need for uproar with much more sophisticated defenses. Giving up repetition compulsion, denial, and a passive-aggressive characterological structure, Marcie began to use the five superior defenses. She synthesized a new way of being in the world, and it paid off. Using *humor* and *anticipation*, Marcie planned carefully to control Jason. She *sublimated* her need for uproar by volunteering to work on a suicide hotline two mornings a week. Knowing we were analyzing Jason's difficulties allowed her to stop talking about him with anyone, including Jim (*suppression*). The church work and hotline kept her mind busy attending to others outside the family—*altruism*.

HAASS is the acronym for the five most sophisticated defenses used to stay out of touch with our unconscious conflicts: humor, anticipation, altruism, sublimation and suppression. No matter how perfectly we were parented or how much therapy we have had, there are always residual conflicts threatening our peace of mind. The conscious ego is fully engaged in keeping us functioning in a complicated world. The repression barrier, made up of our defenses, protects us from battles between the superego and the id.

Humor always encourages everyone as they go through life's trials. The vacuum cleaner monster avoided another tedious discussion about parental expectations in kids' rooms. Not getting defensive by taking children's criticisms seriously allows for harmony in the home. When any of my five children were irritated with me, I would suggest they take me to the new mothers' store. Offering to go pack my bag, I could exit a tense scene. The new mothers' store is where you can leave your old mother and pick out a new one from the shelves. Each mother is clearly labeled with her own characteristics, such as: lets you eat candy all day, does not make you go to bed, lets you play instead of going to school, does not make you clean your room, etc. When my children asked what would happen if they traded me in, whether I'd stay on the shelf in case they decided to reclaim me, I said I hoped so because I loved being their mom, but some other child might come along and select me. For some reason, my kids never got around to taking me to the new mom store! Why argue when humor can put the conflict in a new perspective?

With exercise, plus determined control of her thoughts, Marcie was able to *anticipate* future occurrences and plan carefully. Instead of giving orders to get chores done, Marcie relied on the chart and Jason's desire for toys. Instead of yelling, Marcie trained herself to be quiet and take time before responding.

Altruism means resolving to attend to others. Marcie learned to focus on needs and problems away from her own, rather than perseverate about herself. Loving our neighbors is good mental health.

Sublimation means putting energy into other areas than those we cannot change. In involves disengaging from hopeless tasks and engaging in productive activities. Marcie really enjoyed learning to work with suicidal people.

Suppression simply means not thinking about difficulties we are circumstantially unable to resolve. As Marcie filled her mind with prayer, the old circular ruminations melted away. Obsessing about Jason stopped when she refused to talk about his problems with anyone.

Children Are the Victims

Everyone has a right to harmony. Children are victims in homes where parents argue and yell. They have no power to reduce the tension. School problems, stomach troubles, anxiety reactions, sleep disturbances, nervous tics, asthma, hyperactivity, obstreperousness, panic attacks, headaches, dyslexia, depression, inattentiveness—the list goes on and on, revealing problems youngsters manifest when their homes are tense. Adults are also disturbed mentally and physically when home is a battleground instead of a haven of rest. Adults can do something about the uproar; they are able to decide to stop it by getting professional help, if necessary. Marcie took action. She learned how to keep harmony around her. With courage and steadfast faith, Marcie endured the discomfort of changing the way she was in the world.

God walked with her every step of the way. Marcie was a baptized Christian, dedicated to her Lord. Once she comprehended the marvelous fact that God wanted her to enjoy life, showing forth His glory in her joy and peace that passes understanding, she was able to pray steadfastly for a new life. Repenting of her old ways, she was transformed into a little sister of Christ Himself. She was amazed at her new depth of understanding of Scripture and delighted by her daily conversations with Jesus. "(She) was filled with wisdom, and the grace of God was upon (her)" (Luke 2:40).

Three years after I last saw Marcie, she wrote, "Again, thank you for all that you have done for me. You know I never ever ever could have handled any of this without you. I would have allowed the challenge to destroy me rather than to use it as a tool to grow. I also seek every opportunity to share your light, now my light, with those around me. The Christ light keeps me on my path, and I shine it whenever I can for those around me."

"In your patience possess ye your souls" (Luke 21:19 KJV).

4
Be a Man

MAX

Synopsis: Max, a widower, was terrified of the panic attack he expected to suffer if he refused to marry his present lady friend. A previous attack, brought on by being left by an earlier lady friend, indicated an unconscious conflict over unresolved rage and abandonment fears connected to his dead mother and rekindled when his wife died. Despite the fact of his being a highly successful businessman, community leader, and father, the trauma of his mother's death in childbirth when he was two years old made it impossible for Max to enjoy, not need, women.

Be a Man

Max was fifty-five years old when he came to my office suffering from severe depression. He couldn't sleep or find any meaning in his life. He was frightened of the future and regretful about the past.

To all outside observers, Max should have been a very happy man. He had three grown children who had given him seven grandchildren; all were pursuing successful lives. Max was the vice president of a large, international banking firm. He lived in a lovely house in a prestigious neighborhood—the same home in which he had reared his children. He had many friends in the community. In other words, there was no apparent reason for Max to feel so depressed.

But besides feeling depressed, Max was afraid. He was afraid that he was going to lose control of his mind and go into a major tailspin. It had happened to him once before; he had almost required hospitalization. I asked Max what it was that had precipitated the previous nervous breakdown. He explained that after his wife died, he had fallen in love with a beautiful woman, Wendy, who dumped him after six months. He became so agitated after that abandonment he couldn't work, sleep, sit still, or eat. Prescribed medication soothed him sufficiently so he didn't have to be hospitalized, but he was really frightened that the panic would reoccur.

I asked him about his wife, Rita. They'd been married for twenty-four years. She had been a very high-energy person who not only managed the home and raised the children, but also was very active in community affairs. When she died after an eighteen-month battle with breast cancer, he felt both loss and relief. He hadn't experienced the state of agitated depression he felt later when he was jilted. He hypothesized that possibly it was because the cancer was so exhausting for all of them that when Rita finally died, they were relieved to know she was out of her misery. Max was a staunch Presbyterian. He believed she had gone on to be with the Lord and expected to see her again when he died.

I asked, "Why do you feel afraid?"

"I am living with a woman who wants to marry me. I can't set a date. She's very upset."

"Tell me about your relationship."

"During the first year, it was absolutely delightful. However, once we decided to get engaged, she moved into my family home. Our friendship changed. She supervised me intensively, suggesting how I ought to dress, spend my time, manage my business, and handle my grown children. She frequently says that if I want her to marry me, I will have to straighten out this or that situation, or behave in a certain way."

Angie had never been married before. She was vice president of an insurance company, a high-powered business woman with strong opinions about how people should function. When Max suggested that he wasn't terribly interested in what she thought was right, that he had done things the way he did them for fifty-five years, and in his family, the way he did things was right, she'd get very angry and say he was just trying to upset her by arguing.

I asked, "How was it with your wife? Was Rita also bossy?"

He replied, "Oh yes, of course. She was a real perfectionist; she liked things done in a way that wouldn't embarrass her with the neighbors."

He complied with her wishes because he couldn't argue. Rita would stop any discussion by saying, "It's best for the children," or "Everybody does it this way. Why are you being so pig-headed?"

Max adapted to her wishes. It wasn't very difficult because he was working twelve to fourteen hours a day trying to make enough money to guarantee a secure future and give his youngsters a college education. He hadn't had as much time at home or traveling with Rita as he now had with Angie.

I asked Max how it had been when he was little. His mother had died in childbirth when Max was two years old. His father's sister moved in to raise the five children. The oldest girl was eleven. His aunt was a good woman though very stern and stiff. She did her duty as she believed God wanted her to do it. There wasn't much laughter around the house. I asked Max if he ever experienced missing his mother.

"No, I can hardly remember her."

His father worked hard as a coal miner to support his family. He was not available emotionally for his sons and daughters. He didn't have time to go see their ball games or money to take them out to a show. After work, Max's father came home, washed, ate his supper, and fell into bed—day after day after day.

Still Looking for His Mother

Max was only eighteen when he got married. Rita was a friend in high school. They married as soon as they graduated. He met

Wendy, the lady whose jilting led to the overwhelming anxiety reaction, within two weeks of his wife's death, though they didn't start dating for six months. Her interest, however, was perfectly clear from the first meeting; she was eager to spend as much time with him as possible. She finally left him because he would not set a date for their wedding. I asked about the nature of their relationship.

He replied, "She was a very domineering woman. She knew what was best for me. She took me shopping and bought good clothes, which I needed, as I really have no fashion sense. She redecorated my house so that I wouldn't have to live with so many mementos of my dead wife. Wendy told me how to nurture the children through the loss of their mother." Max smiled, "She was quite a gal. She knew the right way to do everything."

An unconscious conflict was making it impossible for Max to tie the bonds of matrimony. He was caught in a Catch-22 because he needed a woman. But there is a difference between needing and loving a woman. Adult men who individuated from their mothers at the proper developmental stage love women for their unique selves. Max was still looking for his mother to continue caring for him—a need that had been prematurely terminated by her death. The shock of abandonment had been so great that his Junior made a life-long decision to keep a woman at all costs. At age two he was not potent enough, big enough, wise enough, or strong enough to keep his mother. So he decided that when he grew up, he would see to it that he was never abandoned again. Though his aunt had done the best she could, a child of two needs the person with whom he's bonded. His whole capacity to individuate from the original situation with his mother was curtailed. Max never separated from his mom. She left him.

In psychological jargon, we call the period between ages eighteen months and thirty-six months the time of *rapprochement*. It's a time when a toddler leaves his mother's side to play for a little bit and then rushes back, practicing individuating from the dyadic situation. If a little boy can't do that, he's caught forever between needing his mother and needing to be his own person. When he's bonded with a woman, he wants to be free. When he's free, he's frantic to be attached. If you've ever seen a frightened two-year-old left by his mother in Sunday school, you can feel the bleak despair through his tears. He is terrified his mother will not return. When she comes back after church, he's overjoyed. The needed person, who makes him safe, is once again within his reach. He can start playing if she's nearby.

A child smothered by too much closeness with his mother can also be kept from learning about the world. His natural adventurous explorations of objects and heights can be squelched by an ever-present, overly anxious parent. He feels overwhelmed and consumed by her constant admonitions to be careful. There is no chance to form his own conclusions about a toy because she shows him how to use it and put it neatly away. Her opinions about people and places are constantly drummed into his ears. He feels helpless and stupid.

Max had tolerated being attached to his opinionated wife because his manhood, his competence, and his independence were fed by success in the working world. As he rose into positions of power in the company, he knew he was intelligent. When people came to him needing his counsel, it reinforced his sense of being a strong, independent man who could handle anything that came his way. And his rapprochement needs were met because his wife was there every evening when he came home, fixing a good dinner and nurturing his children. He felt he was safe. Then she died, just like his mother. Coping with that, even though in a real way he was glad she was released from her agony, had left him vulnerable to a second abandonment a year later.

I Can't Stand the Loneliness

Now Max was afraid that if he didn't get married to Angie, she too would abandon him and he would flip out. The previous time the doctor had given him antianxiety medication and he had his high-powered job. Now he was semiretired. He didn't have the antidote of work to distract him from his fears.

I said, "Max, be a man. Get up on your own two feet and learn to live life without a woman. When you need a woman, that's not really love. That's need. Agape love requires that you are perfectly able to self-soothe and self-stimulate. Then you can love a woman purely, just because she is there, not because you need someone to take care of you."

"I can't stand the loneliness."

"What is loneliness? I've never experienced it so tell me what it is."

"You've never experienced loneliness?"

"No, never. What is it?"

"Well," he replied, "it's a frantic feeling that you've got to talk to somebody, that you can't relax unless someone is at the other end of the telephone or willing to go out to dinner."

"Max, that's using people. That's not the perfect freedom our Lord came to give us. You're telling me that you have to keep folks around because you're afraid to be by yourself."

"Yeah, I guess that's it. I really am afraid to be by myself. It makes me nervous."

"Well, then," I said, "there is not a better time than the present to start learning to like your own company."

"How do I do that?"

"Very carefully. Spend time alone. Enjoy visiting with Angie. But also enjoy time when you are able to listen to the rhythms of your own body and quietly talk to God."

"Oh!" he exclaimed. "Is that the secret? I've never felt that I had a very deep relationship with God."

I grinned. "I'm not surprised. It sounds to me as though you've always kept people around. Their noise and needs make it very difficult for God to get through."

Max asked Angie to move out of his house the very next week. She wanted assurances that their relationship wasn't over. He told her he wasn't sure. He felt he needed to get to know himself, get balanced on his own two feet, find out who he was, alone. Angie was not pleased. She ranted and raved and told him he was ruining her life, that she had wasted eighteen months on their relationship, believing that they would be married.

I had urged Max to call me every night so that, in case he started to panic, I could perhaps stabilize him without the use of medication. The final week was very difficult while Angie was getting her things together and arranging to move out of the house. Angie wouldn't tell him where she was going. She even hinted she might commit suicide. However, Max had heard my urgings about becoming a man, about loving and not using people. With my daily encouragement, he held steady.

Angie moved out and we waited. Max was still convinced that he'd go into a panic reaction. I was pretty convinced by this time that he wouldn't, that our relationship was strong enough to prevent the abandonment reaction.

In psychoanalytic jargon, I was his transitional object, something like Linus' blanket, or a little kid's teddy bear. It's the object or person endowed by the child's imagination with the mother's presence, which allows him to feel safe even though she's not there. If you've ever tried to take a transitional object away from a young child, you know how they are passionately attached. In the "Peanuts" cartoon strip, Linus sits in front of the washing machine, sucking his thumb, waiting for his blanket to reappear. He can't play or talk or move until he is sure the object is safely back in his hands. That's the way infants feel about their mothers. During the rapprochement period, as mother spends more time away from the child, the transitional object stands for mother and reduces abandonment anxiety.

You might say that I was substituting myself for Max's women, helping him manage his anxiety about the loss of Angie. You'd be perfectly right. That's precisely what I was doing. The difference between his attachment to me and to any other woman is that I'm a therapist. I continually monitored and interpreted his feelings about me, giving him a handle on Junior's inappropriate reactions versus his adult, appropriate feelings. I taught him which of his inner states were part of his mature self and which were residual from Junior. That's called analyzing the transference, the transference meaning the relationship with the therapist.

Max asked me how he should spend his time after work now that Angie was gone. I suggested he go to church and meet some people whose lives are passionately involved with the Lord. He thought that was a super idea as he hadn't made time in the past to study God.

I've Learned to Be a Man

Three months later, Max told Angie that he had decided, for the time being, he was not going to get married to anyone. A whole new life had opened as he began to know himself and talk with Jesus.

Max continued to date a number of women but he was very careful not to get into intense relationships. He decided to avoid sexual encounters. If any woman was clearly predatory, he gave her a wide berth.

Four months later one of his children called up and thanked me for being a miracle worker. I asked what it was that I had done and he replied, "I don't know, but my father is a new person. He laughs a lot now. He plans adventures alone and with companions—one of us or one of his friends. He doesn't get depressed anymore. We are very grateful." I said that I was delighted because his father was a wonderful man.

I didn't hear from Max for four years. Then he called me one winter morning just to tell me that he was alive and well on planet earth. He was dating an attractive woman he thought he might marry. He said, "Georgie, I enjoy her but I don't need her. Don't worry. I've learned to be a man."

Max

Conclusion: Therapists often probe for unconscious rage when severe depression is presented by the patient. Inexplicable fear and deep regret may have unconscious roots, as well.

For Max, the loss of his mother at a critical stage in his development was the cause of his rage at her for leaving him, fear of abandonment, and regret that he had missed something precious. A two-year-old cannot understand why his mother is suddenly not there. He's too little to have individuated and learned to be his own person. He feels as if she's been taken away because he was having temper tantrums or saying "no." The sweetness of the breast and the mother's soothing voice are yearned for intensely.

It was so painful, Max had resolved never to feel that despair again. He *repressed* the memories and feelings, allowing his wife, Rita, to care for him, much as his dour, bossy aunt had managed the family. Wendy and Angie were also encouraged by Max to take control over him in personal matters. This *repetition compulsion* defense, repeating the household presided over by his aunt, kept Max safe though dissatisfied. He didn't know that he yearned for his mother's lap—a world irrevocably lost to adults. We have glimpses of it in good companionship, empathic communication, and reciprocal sexual relationships, but never can we recapture that original enmeshed union.

Using me as a transitional object, a stand-in for his mother, Max could complete the interrupted developmental work toward individuation. Together, we could analyze his feelings and identify those that were appropriate to the present situation and those that were reactive to the earlier environment when he was helpless and afraid. The mother's death was much worse for two-year-old Max, who needed her to complete rapprochement, than for the newborn, who never knew her, or the older children who had individuated appropriately.

Max tried to make me take over his life and tell him what to do. He felt compelled to repeat his role as a helpless, stupid little boy with all women. I was able to point out that behavior every time it surfaced. He learned to stop giving away power. After all, he was a very successful businessman, not a small boy. He could sort out what he liked and didn't like in clothes, furnishings, and social events.

It is not my right as a therapist to discuss the morality of Max having sexual relationships outside of marriage, unless he is concerned about it. I am not a pastor charged with overseeing the morality of his flock. If a person is homicidal or suicidal, I must report him to the authorities; but otherwise, behavior is not for me to judge. If a client wants to act differently, I can give him ways to change. Usually the roots of inappropriate behavior are buried deep in Junior, which is why a diet or exercise program doesn't last for more than a few weeks. Trying to change the way we think or react depends on a trusting relationship with a supportive therapist. If Max had felt judged by me about anything, our journey together would have been severely hampered. To keep my approval, the material he brought to each session would have been slanted. Thoughts, feelings, and actions remain unshared if the therapist criticizes the patient. Max would have studied my opinions to conform as he had conformed to his aunt.

Our God wants us to live out the unique life He envisioned while we were in our mother's wombs. "For you created my inmost being; you knit me together in my mother's womb" (Psalm 139:13). Therapists should not ever clone patients, undermining their individuality. We honor God when we restrain ourselves from giving advice in therapy, in prayer groups, or in casual conversation. Responding to "What should I do?" with "Tell me all the various possibilities," allows the petitioner to make up his own mind. As he talks, he can feel which decision generates the most enthusiasm. We can hear it, too, and be a confirming witness.

Jesus promised the Holy Spirit would bring all things needful to our minds at the right time (John 16:13). He is absolutely trustworthy. We have to be very careful not to get trapped by friends or clients into allowing them to listen to us rather than to Almighty God. "'For my thoughts are not your thoughts, neither are your ways my ways,' declares the Lord. 'As the heavens are higher than the earth, so are my ways higher than your ways'" (Isaiah 55:8–9).

"But ye are a chosen generation, a royal priesthood, an holy nation, a peculiar people; that ye should shew forth the praises of him who hath called you out of darkness into his marvelous light" (1 Peter 2:9 KJV).

5
Enjoy Being Single

ANN

Synopsis: The child buried deep inside this attractive thirty-six-year-old woman wanted to have the intense caring she had experienced from her mother when she was a sick little girl. Ann took very good care of others through listening and gifts, unconsciously hoping she would receive the same support from them. She fell in love with men very like her father, who had been filled with rage and given to explosive outbursts, rather than seeking out loving, stable boyfriends. She found them boring like her ex-husband.

Therapy consisted of helping Ann uncover the unconscious motivations which kept her on the treadmill of romantic excitement and bitter disappointment. New ways of understanding brought new feelings that culminated in a quiet contentment. As we studied Scripture, she became aware that blessed singleness, showing forth the fruits of the Spirit, honored God more than obsessional preoccupation with getting married.

Enjoy Being Single

Ann came to me because she was desperately in love with Timothy, a lawyer who was doing some real estate work for her. She was obsessed with him—with his eyes, his hair, his laugh—and she found excuses to call him whenever possible. She could not get him out of her mind. The obsession had become so severe she was having difficulty sleeping and eating.

Timothy was a divorced man with four children, ages three through eleven; Ann was sure she would be a fabulous mother. Pictures of the children lined her dresser; she knew their individual likes and dislikes. With great difficulty, she restrained herself from going to the store and buying clothes she felt they would enjoy.

Ann was distressed because she couldn't get Timothy out of her mind, and Timothy, though polite to her, had never shown the least romantic inclination in her direction.

I asked Ann about her past experience with men and she said that she'd been married when she was twenty-one for two years to a man who had turned out to be a real jerk. His main fault seemed to be that he was boring. When she suggested that they separate, he didn't seem to have any objection; so, without regrets on either side, they divorced. Her major concern, in fact, was the censure of good church folks who told her that she was breaking God's law by getting a divorce. Since then Ann had dated a number of different men for short periods of time, but had never really found anybody very interesting until she met Timothy eighteen months ago. Now he was a major preoccupation.

Ann was the oldest of four children, planned for and dearly beloved. Her father worked in the aircraft industry, supervising an assembly line. At three, when Ann developed infantile diabetes, her mother took her to a Chicago hospital. Her mother's life, before Ann's illness, had centered on her own parents and on keeping a nice home for her husband. It must have been traumatic for her to travel out of California for the first time with a critically ill three-year-old. Furthermore, she had been five months pregnant. Ann could remember sitting in the middle of the bed, delighted by the attention from all the doctors and nurses. She could not recall her fears, the needles, the tests, nor her young mother's anxiety; the defense of repression had blocked such thoughts from her memory.

They flew home two months later and subsequently Ann's mother gave birth to another little girl. Trips back and forth to a nearby hospital kept the family financially strapped and deeply concerned about Ann's survival. Daily shots and attention to her food intake were necessary. Ann grew to like the attention, accepting it in some ways as compensation for the physical discomfort she had to endure. When an insulin crisis occurred, the whole family responded to the life-threatening danger; racing to the emergency room was routine.

Two younger brothers were born, adding to her mother's workload. As Ann matured, she became responsible for the daily management of her body. The three younger children competed for attention from her parents, leaving Ann with the daily discomfort of the disease and progressively less attention.

Ann's father responded to the diabetes with rage, causing him to withdraw from her. He couldn't stand being healthy while his beloved little girl had such a serious illness. Ann desperately needed his attention while her mother was preoccupied with the young ones. Instead, he worked twelve-hour days to support his growing brood. He was adamantly opposed to his wife's working. A deeply religious man, her father saw to it that his family attended a local Baptist church twice on Sunday and every Wednesday evening. When he became overtired from work and stress, he exploded angrily. Ann remembers cowering during her father's periodic temper tantrums.

Ann's mother responded to her husband's emotional outbursts with agitation and depression; she became more and more overwhelmed by life. Ann experienced her as constantly running around trying to keep everybody happy, desperate to placate her husband by keeping their four children in line. Her mother's fearfulness and general indecisiveness led Ann to believe that a woman needed a man no matter how abusive he was toward her.

I asked Ann to come into psychotherapy with me once a week for a year because her diabetic specialist told me she was fighting a serious form of the disease and must be as stress-free as possible. The obsession was dangerous. Intervention was needed to untangle Ann's infantile conflicts against which the defense of obsessing about Timothy was being used. Rationally, Ann knew Timothy wasn't interested in her, and she knew she did not have the strength to care for his children. His temperament was much like her dad's; she didn't want to repeat her mother's anxious self-sacrifice.

Ann's daily life was rather simple. She worked as a receptionist in a dentist's office. By the time she returned home from work, she was very tired. On the weekends she tidied up her apartment and prepared her clothes for the next week. She was aware she had less energy than most people. Ann would have liked to go to church Bible studies, dances, and other activities enjoyed by young women of her age.

I suggested that she block the obsession immediately by cognitive behavior modification techniques, turning her mind away from her hopeless yearning for Timothy. Every time he or his children came into her mind, she was to recite a Psalm or exercise physically. In the beginning, this was extremely difficult. Slowly she gained control over her thoughts. Family life and holidays were particularly difficult because Ann liked to bake and decorate a home. Giving up thinking about Timothy meant giving up thinking about that kind of a life. In therapy, we had to do some real grief work.

Savoring the Attention

A good therapist usually is able to ascertain a person's main unconscious conflicts within the first two hours of conversation. It takes a lot longer to do the therapy. After the first two sessions, I pictured Ann's infancy and early years, realizing she liked being the center of attention. Most little girls do; but in her case, because of the diabetes, she had received a great deal of extra attention. Her mother had to watch over her very carefully even after the birth of her younger sister.

In normal development, when a youngster reaches eighteen months, her mother's passionate, biological attachment to the infant begins to wane in preparation for the next child. This occurs even if a new sibling never joins the family. By three, most little girls have individuated from their moms. Their dyadic relationship (two-person intimacy called bonding) is over. They turn to their fathers to fill in the gap left by mother's disengagement and, if the father is available, they develop a healthy gender identity and capacity to relate comfortably to boys when they are teenagers. All of this normal growth was disturbed by Ann's sickness.

The excitement of that trip to Chicago, including her pleasure in being the center of a great deal of attention, was destroyed by the birth of her little sister when they returned to Southern California. There, in the beloved mother's lap, was an interloper taking the attention she herself craved.

Ann's father was not available to assuage her pain. He tried to do his best but he was not able to be emotionally available for his daughter. Many men with a sick or handicapped child turn from that flawed human being to worry about the future and finances. They cannot stand the distress of being well while their little one suffers. A normal relationship is disrupted because of the father's mixed emotions when with his child.

I knew in the first two sessions that Ann was arrested at the three-year-old level. She presented charmingly; she was funny, bright, and entertaining. Every hour I spent with her was delightful because of her winsome ways. Ann loved to bring me presents and asked solicitously after my health. I could almost see, in the patient sitting in my office, the little girl sitting on a bed in that Chicago hospital. I hypothesized that Ann's obsession with Timothy covered her rage at not being the center of attention. She worked very hard at being endearing and attractive. Her clothes were well-chosen, her accessories matched, and her makeup was skillfully done. She went out of her way to be friendly and gracious. Among her friends she was known as a counselor because whenever anybody had a problem, they went to Ann for her listening ear and good advice. She knew she was very important to her family and friends but she wanted a significant other.

Yearning for a Prince to Come

In America today the possession of a significant other is seen as our birthright. Little girls grow up believing that they will one day light up someone else's life and that his attentive concern for them will last. This expectation is a real evil perpetuated in our society. It sets people up to hope for something that's only temporarily available, if at all. From the time we leave the dyadic relationship with our mother, we must learn to support ourselves. Our fathers help turn us into little girls or little boys who are distinct individuals, not infants attached to our mothers. But we are really on our own. The pain of losing the closeness with our mothers, combined with the myth of our society about togetherness, leads people to yearn for the day when their prince or princess will come. *The Cinderella Complex* addresses this subject.

The truth is that God didn't arrange His universe so that we could find permanent satisfaction and comfort in any other person. That is not to say that there aren't periods of time when other people can give us insight about Kingdom living. They help us grow and develop. Sometimes we are very close to spouses, parents, children, and friends. But these times always pass, because our God is a jealous God. He is ultimately only interested in our being fully individualized persons enjoying a relationship with Him.

Fritz Perls, the founder of Gestalt therapy, said that we all have expectations about something every minute of every day. We expect our hair to curl in a certain way. We expect our clothes to fit in a certain way. We expect our breakfast to taste a certain way. We expect our car to perform in a certain way. We expect the weather to be as we want it to be. We expect our fingernails to grow in a certain way. We expect our joints to feel a certain way. We expect people to treat us in a certain way. We expect our boss to appreciate us in a certain way. We expect the movie to entertain or enlighten us. In other words, all day long, every day, we naturally have expectations.

Fritz Perls said that if these expectations aren't met, we get resentful. We resent the fact that our clothes feel tight, that our hair doesn't curl, that our breakfast wasn't very satisfactory, that our boss doesn't appreciate us, that our car doesn't run properly, that the weather is gloomy, or that our friends don't respond to us the way we want them to respond. He said that resentment is sin. It's what makes mental illnesses, the feelings of dissatisfaction and discomfort in the world. Perls went on to say that if our expectations aren't met for too long a time, the resentment turns to guilt. We feel guilty for having asked our father to give us the quality of relationship we wanted. We feel guilty for expecting our boss to notice the outstanding work we're doing. We feel guilty for wanting our friends to be supportive.

Ann suffered guilt because she really wanted to be happily yoked with somebody else. Despite her physical limitations, she believed she could manage a home and children. Having all her life been encouraged to take good care of herself so that the disease wouldn't ravage her body quite so quickly, Ann did not have any comprehension of what it takes to manage a family, especially a family with children. She pictured fires in the hearth, popcorn, and sweet children sitting around being grateful for delicious little meals that she had cooked. Ann's own mother had worked so hard to keep the children in line to forestall the father's explosive rage, Ann really didn't have any idea of how managing a family could be stressful. She believed Norman Rockwell's picturesque propaganda, and Grandma Moses' saccharine view of life.

Biblical Role Models

I told Ann to enjoy being single. I told her that God wanted intense dialogue with her and that the responsibility of a family might be too physically taxing. I told her to begin to dwell on all the wonderful blessings she had as a single woman. She could come and go as she wished. She could find the food in the refrigerator that she had left there the night before. She had the luxury of long, quiet evenings and weekends in which to enjoy God.

Ann and I did a lot of talking "demythologizing" the family as a source of happiness. We had to undo some theological training she had absorbed. She had been taught that every person had another person waiting for them, that God intended all Christians to be joined as one flesh, that for each Eve, there was an Adam, so to speak. Salvation was for men and women together, not as separate individuals. When I pointed out that Jesus and Saint Paul lived as single men, as had many other men and women called blessed by God despite their lack of nuptial bliss, she began to revise her thinking.

We worked closely with Junior through dreams, helping her get in touch with primitive feelings. The pleasure of being closely connected to mother when she was an infant had left her with a great yearning to be that closely connected to somebody else in her adult life. The extraordinary attention that the diabetes had brought to the little girl, curtailing independence because of her need to depend upon adults for daily medicine and monitored nutrition, interrupted the normal developmental course. She got in touch with rage at her father for not being there, creating an attraction to angry men who are unavailable. Timothy was exactly the type of person Ann sought. His anger was available and he frequently exploded. Many attorneys use this capacity to feel and express anger usefully in their work, but it's hard on relationships.

She became aware of feelings about her mother being fragile and dependent upon her father. She discovered that she believed women couldn't make it in this world without men. As we talked, little Ann began to have a more realistic view about how the world operates.

Within six months of the beginning of therapy, Ann ceased being obsessional about Timothy and was busily organizing herself to live as a single woman. She now accepted she didn't have the strength to raise an infant. Taking on other people's children as a stepmother is difficult for the strongest individuals. She still wished for a Mr. Right with whom she could live a peaceful, comfortable life. However, the phrase, "in all things God works for the good of those who love him" (Romans 8:28), began to assume a new meaning as she counted her daily blessings.

Last week, Ann celebrated her fortieth birthday. She called me to bring me up-to-date. Her job is still interesting and consumes most of her strength. Several men have taken her out recently. She's enjoyed their companionship but is perfectly sure that her life satisfaction does not depend upon marriage. She said to me, "If God wants me to be married, He'll make that happen. I don't have to worry about it anymore." Her diabetes is under control, though her eyes are slowly failing. She accepts the possibility that she may be blind someday; she makes jokes about it. Encouraging others with diabetes has become a great source of pleasure, especially those who are losing their eyesight.

I was privileged to give Ann permission to enjoy being single. In accepting solitary life, she has found that her relationship with God has deepened immeasurably. She really can say with the psalmist, "The Lord has done great things for us and we are filled with joy" (Psalm 126:3).

Ann

Conclusion: Certain therapeutic concepts used by mental health professionals have been discussed in this case history. It might be useful to define those concepts using illustrations from Ann's story.

Obsessions are thoughts which constantly reoccur. They are hard to banish from our thinking, sometimes even interfering with our jobs. They are defenses against an internal conflict in the unconscious. There are age-appropriate developmental obsessions, such as a boy and his bicycle, a girl and her high school sweetheart. These defend against the conflict between wanting to stay a child and wanting to become one's own person, not needing the parent—the individuation crisis.

Allowing Ann to Grieve

Ann's obsession about Timothy and his children was fruitless. He wasn't interested in her. She didn't have the strength to manage a household with four children. Ann's unconscious wish was to marry an angry man, like her father, and make him into a loving, supportive person, like her mother. That's a hopeless wish. We cannot change people through marriage. Developmentally appropriate obsessions lead to learning about ourselves and the world. The boy's obsession with his bicycle leads to mastery which increases his ability to rely on his own body and mind. The girl's crush on her sweetheart helps her prepare to leave the family and join a husband in the future.

Grief work must be done whenever a patient gives up an unconscious belief or behavior. Ann's hope to be able to establish the kind of home she had as a child (with two differences—a confident, adored wife, and a kind, patient husband) had to be abandoned. The Lord our God might at some time give her just such a home, but not when the man she chose to love was as hostile and impatient as Timothy. Since other men bored her, the grief work for the impossible situation had to be processed. Dr. Elisabeth Kübler-Ross talks about five stages of grief: denial, rage, bargaining, depression, and, finally, acceptance. All are crucial steps. Ann now knows that if she starts to be attracted to an angry man, she must run in the opposite direction, because the attraction comes from Junior who doesn't know much about the real world.

Yearning for Acceptance

To oversimplify developmental stages, let me say that the first eighteen months of an infant's life are spent in a very close union with the mother or mothering person. The union is so close that the baby doesn't know that they are separate individuals. He believes his mother feels everything he feels. If he is cold, his mom is cold and she will do something about warming them up. If he is hungry, his mom is hungry and she will get them fed. If he longs to be held by her, she knows it. Therefore, if he doesn't get picked up by the comforting arms, he presumes he's a very bad boy as mommy must be angry with him. No other cause such as phone calls, financial difficulties, marital tension, neighbor problems, or medical distress can be recognized by the baby as reasons for her failure to pick him up. He simply doesn't know about real-world problems. Ann's mom gave Ann a good bonding. She picked her up and was highly empathic—able to understand and respond to the baby's needs.

From eighteen to thirty-six months, the toddler is practicing separating from Mom. He alternates playing independently with sitting on her lap, or saying "no" forcefully while clinging to her leg. By three years of age, the child is aware that he and his mom are separate individuals. If he wants something, he'll have to please the caregiver and make his desires known, usually through language.

As a separate individual, the young child of three is now ready to discover more about the other people around him, especially his father. If permitted, he follows his dad around, prefers his dad to put him to bed, sits on his dad's lap watching TV, and learns games his dad enjoys playing. He also solicits attention from grandparents, neighbors, and siblings, but dad is the most interesting relationship. If dad is not in the home, the child finds substitutes. If dad is home and unresponsive, or actively hostile toward the child, it is interpreted as rejection. The youngster believes for some reason he is bad or unacceptable to his parent. Once again, the little one cannot imagine other reasons why Dad doesn't want to be with him. Work pressures, financial worries, personality problems, or national catastrophes are not processed by the child. All he knows is that his attempts to make contact are rebuffed over and over again. In adult life, this child still yearns to be accepted by those who reject him, just as Ann did. In the unconscious, Ann's obsession to be connected to Timothy covers her rage at her dad for not being available.

When Mom gives birth to another child, her attention is naturally focused on the helpless little one. She resonates accurately with the newborn and so is less available to her older child. Even if she doesn't bear another baby, as a child matures, the mother's complete absorption is replaced by pleasure in seeing her little one become independent. She is comfortable urging him into relationships with others and exploring on his own. This is a biological as well as a psychological process for both mother and child.

If the youngster becomes critically ill, as in Ann's case, the individuation comes to an abrupt halt. Mother must become hypervigilant again, this time to keep the child from dying. Food, activities, medications, and rest need constant surveillance. Ann became angry because she was still being treated like a baby; at three years of age, she wanted to be managing herself. When her developmental need continued to be thwarted, she *identified with the aggressor*—another defense. That means she became hypervigilant about her own health, saw herself as needing protection, and gave up independence for nurturing. Her unconscious belief was that she should be cared for by a significant other because she was not healthy enough to take care of herself.

At about six years of age, a boy or girl begins a new developmental period, called latency, that lasts until about twelve. He stops being very concerned about his relationships with either parent and, instead, focuses on himself. Daily he increases his capacities—physically and mentally. Playing ball, climbing trees, wrestling, reading, computing, mixing strange ingredients—a child become competent. He learns to know himself and begins to master complex tasks. Ann learned to manage her disease, but was tied to her parents by their mutually shared anxiety about the course of her diabetes and their frequent trips to the emergency room. Athletically and scholastically she was handicapped by the lack of energy and time lost from school.

If latency goes well, adolescence is an exciting time of once again exploring relationships. Now peers are the objects of fascination, especially peers of the opposite sex. A teenager who feels good about himself or herself can enjoy the healthy banter and sexual provocation without becoming promiscuous or withdrawn. In embarrassing situations they can laugh and learn rather than feel as if they are stupid or unattractive. Ann had already felt rejection from her father, so this stage was very difficult. She expected to be found unappealing. Despite a heroic endeavor to forestall the inevitable, her attention to the details of her person as well as the supportive skills she learned didn't draw the hoped-for companion. The boys who liked her were boring, even the young man she married. It was like the old joke: "I wouldn't want to belong to any club that would have me as a member."

Healthy adults can enjoy relationships with men and women without having to possess anyone. Living a creative life using their talents and skills is enough. Healthy Christians can dedicate themselves to being "a little pencil in God's hand," as

Mother Teresa put it. Their personalities and abilities are joyfully given to God; in return He fills them with new life. The satisfaction and difficulties of this life are not of concern. Their purpose is to show forth the Christ in their joy and peace that transcends circumstances.

"And the Lord turned the captivity of Job, when he prayed for his friends: also the Lord gave Job twice as much as he had before" (Job 42:10 KJV).

6
Go Play Golf

JONATHAN

Synopsis: Depression brought Jonathan into therapy; his world felt colorless and hopeless. To outward appearance, he had everything—a beautiful woman, a good home and job, friends, a handsome face, and a strong athletic body. Unconscious conflict was analyzed through his dreams. Jonathan gave himself permission to spend his days doing what he enjoyed, freed from the need to suffer. A good transference relationship with his therapist made self-forgiveness possible.

Go Play Golf

Jonathan was a tall, handsome, thirty-three-year-old; golfing was what he liked to do best in the whole world. Whenever he had a little spare time, he went out and hit a few balls. He was good—good enough to win tournaments. Golf was all he could think about.

He lived with his fiancee, Charlotte, in a beautiful home in a desert resort. They were planning to get married in six months and neither wanted to have any children. Charlotte flew all around the country as a personnel manager for an aircraft manufacturer. She was one of the most successful recruiters in the company, very well paid for her efforts.

Jonathan was also a salesman. He sold food products to supermarket chains, traveling by car all through the Southwestern states. He was underwhelmed by his job. Despite having worked at a number of other sales jobs successfully over the years, he really didn't like sales. He didn't like having to get up in the morning, put on his suit, drive to a store, and talk the merchants into purchasing his product. He liked to golf.

Jonathan came to me complaining of depression. He had trouble getting out of bed in the morning. In fact, some days he couldn't get out until noon. He had trouble sleeping at night. He could fall asleep perfectly well, but sometime around two or three in the morning, he'd wake up and not be able to get back to sleep. He lacked energy except when he was on the golf course. He pushed himself to do everything else.

Jonathan was unable to work up any enthusiasm about the future. He couldn't imagine ever enjoying working. It was as if the world were gray. Nothing meant anything to him anymore. He wondered if he had some physical problems. The doctor had declared him a perfect specimen and suggested he go see a psychologist. He was not eager to take any antidepressant medication because it might throw off his golf game. That was the one thing he loved.

I said, "Go and play golf."

He replied, "I'd love to but I have to contribute my fair share to our household expenses."

"Well then, become a pro," I suggested. "Give lessons and play in tournaments and golf will support you."

Emphatically he responded, "Gosh, there are hundreds of guys out there trying to be pros. I'd never make it. I'm not that good."

"Oh, stop it, Jonathan; you're just defeating yourself! If the only thing in the world that you have enthusiasm for is golf, then go and play golf.

"Enthusiasm is one of the ways that God talks to us. If He gives us a burning desire for something, I think we'd better go do it. The Greek root words for enthusiasm are *en theos*, meaning God in us."

Jonathan was not a religious man. His mother had been an extremely pious woman, a staunch Lutheran from upstate New York who dragged her children to church for every weeknight activity and twice on Sunday. Jonathan hated it. He and his two sisters grew up resolving never to set foot inside any kind of Christian church again.

Jonathan believed God decreed a number of impossible rules, punishing with hellfire the smallest infraction. He wanted none of that! If Jesus represented God, then he wasn't interested in Jesus either. He wouldn't worship such a pig-headed, opinionated, punitive deity.

Golf, the Forbidden Pleasure

During our third session, I asked Jonathan about his family life. He said he had always felt that his two sisters were preferred by his mother. He was aware of her confusion about how to raise a boy. She seemed to be in constant distress over his messy ways, loud noises, rambunctious play habits, torn clothes, sweaty socks—his very maleness. The general feeling he got was that girls prefer things neat and tidy, doing things the right way; boys were sort of all elbows and knees.

I asked how he got along with his dad, and he replied, "Not very well."

His dad had been a salesman. He worked very hard and had been gone a good bit of the time. His mom and dad never showed any affection to each other, never a hug or a wink.

Jonathan started to play golf when he was in high school. His mother disapproved violently because the major tournaments were on Sunday. He disobeyed his mother and played golf despite her vehement opposition. College was made possible with a golfing scholarship, but he had never really thought he could make a living doing what he loved.

I saw Jonathan every week for eight months. During that time, we did some dream work to help Junior get over his belief that when boys were being boys, something was wrong. He had come to that opinion, obviously, through his mother's feelings about masculinity. It oozed over into his pleasure in golfing. As long as golf was a masculine activity disapproved of by his mother, he could play. In fact, he could relish the individuation excitement of going against his mother's wishes. Doing the forbidden always produces an adrenalin rush. No real man wants to do what his mother desires. "Up with golf; down with church" was Jonathan's motto.

However, playing golf full-time was not proper or appropriate. Mother taught him to work at a job he disliked all day to have a little bit of time in the late afternoon to do what boys want to do —play. Jonathan could not individuate himself from his enmeshment with his mother enough to make an adult decision about his life's work. He was trapped.

We were able to disengage Junior from believing that becoming a golf professional was forbidden, something God and Mother had decreed along with the Ten Commandments. After several months of hard practice, a country club hired him to teach golf. I can't begin to describe Jonathan's joy when he called me to say he'd been accepted. Charlotte was terribly pleased as well; she had been really worried about Jonathan's pervasive depression.

There Is a God

The last time I heard from Jonathan, he had been working as a golf professional for a year. He was absolutely delighted with everything. Color and hope had returned to his life.

He said, "Georgie, I'm beginning to believe that maybe there is a God in the heavens after all."

Surprised and pleased, I replied, "Hey, Jonathan, what brought you to that position?"

"Because I'm free. You said 'Go and do what you need to do; it's God prompting you when you have this much enthusiasm for something.' I went and I'm doing it. If I hadn't met you, I'd still be selling cake mixes and breakfast cereals up and down the dusty roads of the Southwest."

Because I gave him permission to freely follow his heart's desire, Jonathan began to revise his opinion of the Lord of the universe. I believe he'll come to a personal knowledge of Jesus in the near future. My job is not to preach. That's for other folks. My purpose is to call people into the full dimension of their humanity as beloved sons and daughters of God.

Jonathan

Conclusion: Setting captives free is one of the great joys of a therapist's life. Jesus told us that we would do what He did and more (John 14:12). He claimed He'd set the captives free when He quoted Isaiah after He came out of the desert (Luke 4:18). When he said, "Your sins are forgiven" to the paralytic man lowered before Him on the mat (Matthew 9:2), He gave Jonathan permission to play golf. His blood shed on Calvary forgave Jonathan from his assumed wickedness in playing eighteen holes instead of going to church. His willingness to leave His mother set the example so Jonathan could abandon his mother's ways. His wandering lifestyle, instead of doing the expected carpentry, gave the answer to all those who leave jobs to be about their Father's business.

I'm not suggesting that golf is better than sales. There is no way we can come to such a determination. But for Jonathan, golf was better than sales because he was alive and free on the greens. Jonathan went against his mother's wishes to play in tournaments; he was in his element, masculine and independent.

Sweet reason would suggest that since he loved golf and hated sales, Jonathan didn't need therapy to find his occupation. Unfortunately, our behavior and decisions are largely controlled by our unconscious, not our rational mind. *Repetition compulsion* (remember that defense?) suggests the same conflicts occur in adult life as occurred in childhood. Jonathan felt depressed and bored at home and church. He escaped into golf. My job was to sort through Junior's thoughts and feelings to discover the situation he was forced to repeat. Living with a powerful business woman, Charlotte, who loved spending time on her job and prospered through hard work, reminded him of his mother's devotion to the church and Lutheran promises of prosperity for the faithful. His unconscious didn't doubt that living a devoted Christian life, as defined by his pastor, was the right way, insuring a good life on this side and heaven on the other. Junior felt very guilty because he had deliberately sinned over and over, golfing on Sunday. Junior believed such willful breaking of the fourth commandment was unforgivable.

As an unrepentant sinner, Jonathan's unconscious condemned him to boring work, to changing jobs frequently so he couldn't attain power or prestige, to never having children to fill his quiver (Psalm 127:5), and to always being second best to a strong woman. If Charlotte had left him, Jonathan would have had to find another charming go-getter to overshadow him. Anytime a chance at financial success or a promotion appeared, he would have to change jobs. In popular literature, this is sometimes called "fear of success." He had already tried and judged himself; the verdict was guilty. Only girls, like his sisters, or good religious men who followed the Law exactly had a right to happiness—to living in the land flowing with "milk and honey" (Exodus 3:8).

As we talked about all these unconscious strands causing his depression, Jonathan began to understand more and more clearly how he had sabotaged himself. The scriptures about Jesus dying for us while we were still in our sins (Romans 5:8) returned to him allowing self-forgiveness. Because I affirmed him without condemnation, though he knew I was a Christian, he could begin to internalize a loving God who longs for His children to enjoy life. His athletic prowess was seen as a good gift from his Heavenly Father, not the skills of a bad boy. As I delighted in his growth, Jonathan began to understand how much God yearns to have us each reach maturity (Ephesians 4:14-16), becoming ourselves "in truth relentlessly" as Dr. John Finch puts it.

Experiencing Freedom

The point is not whether Jonathan remains a golf professional the rest of his life. Having experienced the freedom to follow his own enthusiasm, he may well choose another career demanding less physical exertion and offering superior financial reimbursements. It doesn't matter what he does. What matters crucially is his investment in his own creativity and growth. I believe he will find Jesus more and more as he goes through life, because Scripture is deep in his heart. His mother's gift of exposure to the Word, though rejected by the boy, will become the rock on which the man will stand.

Along the way, Jonathan's courtesy and kindness will bless many lives. Though he isn't professing the Lord Jesus at the moment, he will live a graceful life from having spent so many years studying His ways. God will raise up others to witness His steadfast love to Jonathan, as He produced me at a critical time. One day Jonathan will turn and say, "Abba, Father."

"For if these things be in you, and abound, they make you that ye shall neither be barren nor unfruitful in the knowledge of our Lord Jesus Christ" (2 Peter 1:8 KJV).

7

You May Not See Your Grandchild

THEA

Synopsis: Michelle, a thin twenty-year-old bulimic, came to an anorexic-bulimic group to work on her compulsive behavior. The vomiting stopped as she gained self-confidence. Bingeing and purging only occurred after she talked to her mother, Thea. As Michelle's personality unfolded, she was able to marry and become pregnant. Vomiting put the fetus at risk. Therapy with Michelle and her mother stopped the bulimia. By the time the baby was born, they were able to communicate.

You May Not See Your Grandchild

I didn't meet Thea until a year and a half after I met her daughter, Michelle. Michelle came to the group that met every Friday night in my office to see if she could get control of the bulimia that was devastating her life. She'd dropped out of college after two years because she didn't have energy left over for studying. Michelle had curly yellow hair surrounding her sweet face. Because of the vomiting, her face was drawn and pale with dark circles under her eyes. When she smiled, she was lovely but most of the time she stared solemnly.

In the group we talked about dreams. Their vomiting, taking laxatives or diuretics, how much they had eaten or how much money they had wasted on binge food was of no interest to me. Reinforcing their negative behavior with attention was counterproductive. Such discussions usually dissolved into "my behavior is grosser than your behavior."

One person told a dream. Then we went around the room so that each individual could share how the dream made them feel and what it reminded them of in their lives. Then the dreamer shared his or her feelings and associations. My belief is that the reason otherwise normal, healthy, bright human beings are so crazily self-abusive to their bodies, their careers, their capacity to study, work, and love, has to do more with how they felt about themselves when they were very tiny infants than with later traumas. I wanted to get to know the infant inside each anorexic or bulimic; the quickest way was through their dreams.

Most of the time Michelle sat very quietly, though she participated when her turn came, sharing feelings and memories. She felt that nobody was interested in her thoughts, opinions, and tastes because her mother never listened to her. Her mom is a charming, articulate woman with strong judgments. Michelle was shy and quiet. Throughout her childhood, her mom talked for her, even answering questions directed at Michelle. Week by week in therapy she grew stronger, more aware of the real Michelle. She could say, "This is me. This is what I believe and feel and see and enjoy." As she strengthened, the bulimia became less and less of a compulsion.

Filling the Emptiness

In reaction to internal panic, bulimics eat as much as a hundred dollars worth of junk food a day. When they are frightened, they can't think of any way to get relief except through their compulsive habit. In this, they are very like cocaine addicts, alcoholics, philanderers, men who have to have sex with one-night-stand pick-ups, people who are compulsive runners even though their knees are giving out, child abusers, and others. Food is the bulimic's main obsession. Fast-food restaurants, donut shops, grocery stores that stay open all night, calories, weight-loss exercise programs, nutrition—bulimics think about food all the time.

Bulimics know how to use food to fill their inner emptiness and how to get it back out again, either by vomiting or laxatives. They are severely damaging themselves. In my experience any attempt to say "stop it" is futile. The anxiety that drives bulimics to binge and purge is so powerful their knowledge of the destructiveness of the habit is of no relevance.

As Michelle began to feel better about herself, she had fewer bulimic episodes. She fell in love with a fine young man. They were married and soon she became pregnant. He came to meetings to encourage her. She was learning that she had power to make things happen. The only time this forward motion was stopped was when Michelle had contact with her mother, Thea. Always, after phone calls or visits home, Michelle became sick again. The bulimia would reappear with a vengeance. She would come to meetings with dark circles under her eyes.

Because she was pregnant, it was crucial that she not vomit anymore. I asked her not to speak to her mother again. Bulimia is a defense against the pain induced by the conflict inherent in trying to grow up and separate oneself from childish dependency on mother. If, in the first year of its life, the infant experiences unempathic nurturing, there will be a dysfunction in the individuation process later on.

Michelle knew that her mother had worked very hard at being a good mother, but somehow she had never been able to get on Michelle's wavelength. Thea was the kind of mother who led Camp Fire groups, gave the best birthday parties, always had the girls dressed perfectly, and worried constantly over everything. But she lacked empathy as to what was going on inside Michelle. She did all the right things, but never found out how her child felt. Thea was the kind of mother who would say, "It's lunch time; eat your lunch."

Michelle would reply, "I'm not hungry."

"Of course you're hungry; it's lunch time!"

Michelle would repeat, "Really, I'm not hungry."

"Of course you're hungry! Don't be a bad girl! You're hurting my feelings after all the work I've done making you a nice lunch."

Thea would say, "Put your sweater on. It's getting dark."

"I'm not cold."

"Of course you're cold; it's getting dark!"

Those contradictions, day after day, left Michelle with an internal emptiness. She didn't know what she thought or felt. Thea was a poor mother. Michelle was able to appear cheerful and adaptive through school, covering her sense of inadequacy. Even when Michelle was in her teenage years, her mother always knew what was right and appropriate for her in clothes, friends, and ideas.

Bulimics often say that their mothers are their best friends. They've never individuated. Whenever they have a decision to make, they listen to the inner voice of mother telling them how to think, dress, and play.

Desperately Connected to Mother

During their childhood, bulimics and anorexics have not evolved unique personalities. They have been overshadowed by dominant mothers. They really don't know "up from down, left from right, good from bad" as group members used to say.

To become a whole person, a holy child of God, each of us has to walk away from Nazareth. "If anyone comes to me and does not hate his father and mother, his wife and children, his brothers and sisters, yes, even his own life, he cannot be my disciple" (Luke 14:26). Passionately connected to God, we must listen to Him deep in our souls, rather than playing the old tapes placed in us by our mothers.

Compulsive people are unable to stand up on their own two feet. They are still trying to get their mothers to see and hear them clearly. Many never get over having their mothers be the major influence in their lives. Sometimes they live with their mothers until they die. They are lonely, unable to make appropriate relationships with their peers. Often bulimics latch onto somebody else who reminds them of their mother, becoming enmeshed with the new person. Or they become enmeshed with their own children, training them to give up their own unique individual personalities for the sake of beloved mother.

The only way to force this growing up is by separating the mother and the adult child. For the sake of the fetus growing in her uterus, Michelle could not afford to vomit anymore. Communicating with her mother threw Michelle into panic. On the outside she became the quiet mouse her mom knew, while feeling frantic internally. To protect the baby, Michelle had to grow up. So I asked her not to make contact with her mom for a year.

As we expected, Thea called up immediately to yell at me over the telephone. She was convinced I was a very bad psychologist. "It is unnatural for a mother to be separated from her daughter for a year."

Calmly I tried to explain the dynamics that were making her daughter so sick, that would injure the infant inside her. Thea would hear none of it. She was absolutely appalled that a professional would suggest anything so bizarre. I asked her to come in for a session; reluctantly, she came.

As we talked, a story of severe early trauma appeared. She had grown up in war-torn France, losing her father when she was ten. Her mother and grandmother struggled to maintain life; food was short, and the Germans cruel. Thea's earliest memories were of neighbors taken away and her family's constant search for bread. She waited in terror for the knock on the door in the middle of the night. Most French men were deported within six months after the German occupation to work in the war factories. Few of them returned. After Thea's father had been taken away, her mother was left with three small children to support and a grandmother who helped, but was also another mouth to feed. They were always hungry.

When Thea came to the United States as a fifteen-year-old, she was determined that her children would not suffer any deprivations. She wanted a life of freedom and plenty. Thea learned English quickly. She married a fine young man and shortly had two children, Michelle and a younger daughter, Renee. At the time I met Thea, Renee was in serious trouble abusing drugs and alcohol. Still amazed at all the good things in America, Thea couldn't imagine how anybody could be crazily self-abusive, wasting food, money, or themselves on substances.

Thea was good-looking, thin and very attractive. She wore a stylish pantsuit with just the right jewelry and accessories. Her makeup was subtly applied. She talked very fast with a delightful European accent. Anyone who met her would be charmed. Remembering her daughter's pale face with dark circles under her weary eyes, I wished that more of her mother's sparkle and high color was available for Michelle.

Thea talked nonstop in response to my questions, with good stories and humor. She worked with her husband in commercial real estate. With an exquisite home in Santa Barbara and a business that was financially prospering, everything was as it should be. She couldn't understand why Michelle and Renee were both having difficulty as young adults. She told me at length all the wonderful things she had done for Michelle and Renee; the lessons, the trips, the clothes, the parties, the PTA, Camp Fire groups, and the soccer teams. She had been a model mother. Thea was bewildered and angry at her children because they couldn't see their good fortune.

How Can You Hurt Me So?

Thea felt Michelle needed her encouragement and supervision. She enjoyed calling every day to hear the latest news and give advice. Then her daughter joined my group and insisted they speak only once a week. Those weekly conversations became very strained. Thea was seriously thinking about filing a lawsuit against me for alienation of affections.

I told her I really understood how she felt. As a mother of five children, I know the pleasure of keeping in touch. I agreed Thea was a wonderful counselor. I understood why Michelle's friends still turned to her when they ran into difficulties. Her advice was wise and helpful. But Michelle was inappropriately attached. She had to grow up and live an independent life. Thea was outraged. She stomped out of my office.

A week later she asked if they could see me together. I agreed because Michelle wanted the meeting. We arranged for two hours to talk. When they came in, Michelle, who was then about five months pregnant, looked even more withdrawn and browbeaten after their luncheon together. Thea, on the other hand, was radiant. They had talked about the baby. Thea was planning exquisite nursery decorations and furniture. She had given Michelle advice about nursing and caring for the infant. For the first fifteen minutes Thea told me all the things she was planning for her first grandchild and how excited she and Michelle were about the things they could do together. Michelle looked shell-shocked! I knew when they parted company after the session, Michelle would go immediately to binge and purge.

Can you imagine having to figure out some way to say to such a forceful and helpful mother, "It won't do. It won't do at all. You cannot see your grandchild"?

Screwing up my courage to the sticking point, I asked, "Can you see the color of your daughter's face?"

Briskly she replied, "Yes, yes, I keep telling Michelle she should put on a little makeup and eat iron."

"Do you know what your daughter is feeling at this very moment?"

"Of course! My daughter is delighted with all the things I'm going to buy her for the nursery!"

I looked at Michelle, "Would you tell your mom how you're feeling right now?" Michelle was terrified. Without a year of therapy and group work, there is no way that youngster, who had been trained to agree with her mom, could possibly have spoken.

Supported by my presence, Michelle said, "Mom, this is my baby. I want to decorate the nursery the way I want to decorate it. I don't want your advice or money. I want to care for the baby in my own way. I don't want you on the phone every day, or dropping by, telling me what I'm doing wrong. Mom, I have to protect myself."

Thea was dumbstruck. Tears welled in her eyes. "How can you talk to me that way, Michelle? How can you hurt me so much? You know I'm just trying to help you. I want to share our money with you so that you can have an easier time with the baby. How are you and that young student husband of yours ever going to give my grandchild the things he or she deserves? You need me. You need me to help you. You don't know how to raise a baby. You don't know anything about how to take care of yourself. I can't understand why you'd say such terrible things."

Michelle cowered further into the corner of the sofa, wrapping her arms around her legs.

I asked Thea, "Do you see how Michelle looks right now?"

Angrily, she answered, "Certainly. I've told her before not to put her dirty feet on other people's sofas. She's all scrunched up. I don't know what's happening with kids these days! They don't appreciate good things when they get them. If she knew what happened to me when I was her age, she wouldn't behave like this. Why, my goodness, I had to avoid enemy soldiers and beg food during most of my childhood. Michelle has never had a hard knock in her life! She's never known a moment of hunger. She has this disgusting habit, spitting up food bought with our hard-earned money.

"But I'm not going to blame her! I have tried to be a good and faithful mother. Children, nowadays, you just can't believe how ungrateful they are, how much they hurt their parents! My friends and I were just talking about it yesterday, how much this younger generation tries to hurt their parents in one way or another." While she talked, Thea was crying copiously, moving around in her seat, gesturing. She was upset and self-righteously indignant.

My responsibility was to help Michelle understand why she needed distance from her mother. Bulimics haven't separated from the early maternal tapes. As soon as her mother started to talk, I was afraid Michelle would completely forget why she was making her mother so unhappy. Her mind would begin to race, sorting out ways to quiet and comfort her mom. I knew all too well the massive impact of a mother's emotionality on a bulimic. I also knew that, for the sake of the child in Michelle's uterus, individuation needed to happen.

I asked Thea, "Do you know how Michelle feels, listening to you explode?"

Thea replied empathically, "Well, I hope she feels guilty for making me so unhappy!"

I looked at Michelle. Quietly, she said, "Yes, Mom, I feel guilty, but I have to be free. I have to make my own decisions and be my own person." She said this in such a small voice that it was very difficult to hear her. Inwardly I was cheering because Michelle, for the first time in her life, had been able to stand up for herself. My fears were groundless.

The Only Relief Is Vomiting

Thea yelled and cried again. She threatened to have Sacramento revoke my state license to practice psychology. She quoted from books and friends and talked in generalities for another half an hour. We listened.

I then asked, "Do you know what Michelle's going to do when you leave her this afternoon?"

"No."

"She'll need to go vomit. After eating a lot of junk food she'll purge, because your talking like this makes her so anxious she goes into a panic state. The only relief for that panic state is vomiting."

Thea stopped cold in her verbal tracks and shifted gears. "Is that why she vomits?"

"Yes, that's why she vomits. Michelle is overwhelmed by her feelings of love for you and her desire not to have you hurt. She also knows that she has to become her own person. Inside each person is a maturational clock which tells them that, at twenty years of age, they should not be enmeshed with their mothers. Part of Michelle wants to be your little girl again and part of her wants to be free to be herself, to mother her own child and be a wife, in her own way, to her husband. Listening to you go on an emotional rampage puts her under so much pressure she's forced to use her habitual defense, eating and vomiting. Do you know, Thea, what that does to the baby?"

She shook her head.

"A child can be born handicapped, blind, deaf, or developmentally damaged in some way because the mother is crazily self-abusive. For the sake of your unborn grandchild, we cannot afford to have you and Michelle talking to each other."

Thea burst into tears. "After all the sacrifice and hard work, it should come to this! I lose my beloved daughter and am not allowed to see my grandchild!"

"Cheer up. It's only for a short while. When Michelle has grown up inside, then you'll be good friends. You can get together happily when the baby is born if you'll agree to two simple rules."

Thea replied, "Absolutely, anything! I have to see my grandchild."

"Okay, the two rules are 'don't criticize' and 'don't give advice.'"

Predictably, Thea blew up again, ranting and raving for another twenty minutes, declaring that ridiculous. I calmed her down as well as I could and sent them out of my consulting door exactly two hours after they walked in. Michelle looked a little stronger, a little braver, a little more as if she could cope. She was plainly relieved not to have to communicate with her mother until after the birth of the baby.

I Must See My Grandchild

A month later Thea called and asked for another appointment. I said, "Of course, I'd be delighted to see you!" We met one spring afternoon in my office. She started right in telling me that she couldn't possibly abide by those two rules. She had talked to all her friends and read a series of books, which she'd brought along so that I could get a decent education. They all pointed out that the separation was unnatural, particularly during a daughter's pregnancy. They went on to explain how an adult child needs her mother to give advice and gifts when she has her baby. Several of the books, written by Christian authors, dealt with grandparents and their need for a close relationship with grandchildren.

I listened carefully as she shared her concerns with lots of emotion, tears, and waving of the hands. I said, "I know you disagree with me. You are very hurt. I feel your pain at being separated from Michelle at this time in her life. I am fighting for the health of the newborn child and your daughter's mental balance so she can be an appropriate mother."

Thea then looked at me. "Are you saying that I'm not good for my daughter? How do you have the nerve?"

I smiled. "I'm brave when the innocent need protection. I'm telling you what you must do if you want to see your grandchild."

Thea flew into a rage, again, threatening me with dire legal consequences, and stormed out of my office. A month later she was back. She started the hour by saying, "I must see my grandchild."

I replied, "I really understand how you feel."

"I don't think you're right. But the only way I'll get to see my grandchild is by doing what you ask me to do. Teach me how to do it."

Enthusiastically, I replied, "I'd love to."

For several months we met together. I pointed out how she habitually spoke to Michelle in ways which felt like criticisms or advice. For example, she would talk about decorating ideas she had been reading in a book. Michelle would experience that as advice. Thea would discuss what the ladies had been sharing about their children at a luncheon that day. Michelle would experience that as personal criticism.

Thea finally asked, "What am I allowed to talk about?"

"Tell her about the ballet, or the art museum, or the fun adventures you've had traveling. Tell her about your pleasure in gardening and how you enjoy your wonderful husband. Tell her about theories, political and economic. Tell her about God."

Thea looked dubious, "I don't know anything about God. All I know is family."

"I know. In the Bible that's called a 'golden calf.' You are worshiping your family, pouring all your energy into it. The Lord, your God, requires that you come into relationship with Him."

Thea asked, "How do I do that?"

"I'll give you the names of several good spiritual advisers with whom you can talk."

Yearning for Power —and Peace

Often mothers who have had traumatic early experiences are so grateful they can provide a calm, enriched family life for their children, they fail to see the need for individuation. As a little girl,

Thea had yearned for the peace of a good home in a quiet, safe country, far from war. Once this situation was achieved, she had thrown all of her energy into her family. To spare them from any discomfort, she robbed Michelle and Renee of opportunities to make their own decisions and their own mistakes.

Renee responded by turning to drugs; Michelle, to bulimia. Thea had done the best she knew to do. Not going to church kept her from hearing the call of God in her life. She was worshiping her family instead of the Almighty.

Thea had been baptized a Catholic in France, attending mass twice a week with her mother. Then, longing to forget the horrors, she stopped speaking French and attending church. God and war were linked in her mind; her fervent prayers had not brought her father home.

In America, a brand new opportunity opened for those strong and bright enough to grasp it. Thea made the most of her second chance. She prospered, proud of her business acumen. All goals were attained until both children began having severe problems. To help her cope with the restrictions on contact with Michelle, I gave her something else to think about, the most precious gift of all. I reminded Thea of the power that sustained her mother through the bleak years.

Common Sense Is Nonsense

When the baby was a week old, Michelle and Thea came to show her off. She was darling. They were both delighted. Michelle had color in her cheeks and talked positively about the things she was doing to care for Shannon. The little one slept in her bed with them so they didn't need a crib. She bought a chest pack to carry the baby while walking and doing housework because she knew the baby needed to be close to her. I was sure Shannon would teach Michelle how to be a good mother if they were together twenty-four hours each day.

Thea was absolutely thrilled with her granddaughter. She wanted very much to become involved in the daily management of the little one's life. Wisely she held back, allowing Michelle to do her own mothering. She talked about how exciting it was to learn about God, working with a spiritual adviser. She had been studying hard. Cory Ten Boom's experiences rescuing Jews in occupied Holland allowed her to recall painful memories. Cory's absolute faith in God reminded Thea of her own mother's steadfastness. As she studied Bible stories, verses memorized years ago came back.

Several times during the sessions, Thea would say things like "Well, you have to put the baby down for naps some of the time." Then she'd look at me and at Michelle, and say, "Whoops, that's advice, isn't it?" We'd both smile. Our time in therapy had given her a new way to be with her daughter without having to give advice or criticize.

Common sense says that all grandmothers have the right to see their grandchildren. But common sense is often nonsense. Jesus said many things that shocked and surprised His audiences because they weren't common sense. He told people to love their enemies, hate their mothers, sell all they had to the poor, take up their cross and follow Him, become as little children, be born again. These commands are not common sense. Grandchildren do need their grandparents, but only if the grandparents contribute to the mother's peace of mind. If the grandmother is constantly criticizing and antagonizing the mother, it's better if she stays away. I'm happy to report that Thea and Michelle learned how to get along together. Shannon spends lots of time with her doting grandparents.

To make anyone as angry as I had to make Thea is very difficult. Therapists do it in fear and trembling. However, when God directs me to speak a hard word, I have no choice. He knows what everyone needs for salvation. Hallelujah!

Thea

Conclusion: Sometimes people have to be rudely shocked before they'll examine themselves. Thea was comfortable. She'd survived the war and prospered in a new land. She had a good husband, a lovely home, many friends, and two model kids, until they got out from under her control. Then both showed signs of serious mental difficulties; they became crazily self-abusive.

Self-abusive behavior is anger turned upon oneself. No one could fault Thea for her model mothering, least of all the recipients of her efforts. Rage at not being allowed to individuate from her produced compulsive behavior in her children. Thea had advice about everything—school work, friends, clothes, hair, toys, goals, etc.—and she gave it freely. Renee and Michelle talked with her all through their adolescence, because she expected them to answer her questions. Thea believed children should share everything with their mothers, particularly when the mother had dedicated her life to them. Not knowing that openness with Mom during adolescence is maturationally inappropriate, Thea put her youngsters into major conflicts internally.

During her teen years, a girl has to become her own person. Since Mother is powerful and wise, having lived longer, adolescents cling together, giving each other support as they struggle to become independent people. Like the butterfly struggling out of the cocoon, it's hard work to grow up. Having always been a dependent child, turning to mom for everything, getting on one's own two feet is unfamiliar and scary. Evolving an independent identity is the main task of late adolescence. If a strong, charming mother encourages a girl to remain close, she cannot develop her own judgment and taste. She feels like a pale shadow of her mother: less attractive, intelligent, powerful, rich, capable, and desirable.

In much of the world, mothers are worn out or dead by the time their children reach adolescence. (One hundred years ago that was true in America.) Poor food, inadequate medical attention, bad living conditions, and backbreaking work twelve hours a day, seven days a week, wear out human beings. Individuation from parents is not difficult for Third World youngsters. Obviously, the kids are more attractive, stronger, and quicker than physically depleted adults.

In Western Europe and America, grownups live better and longer. Good food, housing, medical care, jobs, and recreation allow human beings to remain energetic mentally and physically.

They have power, money, education, a career, sexual expertise, etc.—all goals which adolescents must achieve.

Thea was a very good woman. She mistakenly thought a human could grow up without frustration, disappointment, and struggle. She believed if parents gave children love and protected them from hardships, secure adults would emerge. She almost suffocated Michelle with advice and gifts. Overwhelmed, Michelle retreated into herself, acting out the individuation conflict by bingeing (taking mother/food in) and vomiting (putting mother/food out), enmeshment and individuation, over and over again.

Mothers feed infants. They bond through physical closeness, especially during nursing. Thea didn't nurse her babies, a decision which disrupted her capacity to empathize with them. She taught them rather than encouraging their initiative. She reasoned for them, deciding which friends, classes, and sports were appropriate. She solved their problems, instead of letting them creatively think up solutions.

Thea's mom had not been empathic with Thea when she was an infant. Her self-concern, before the war, focused on her comfort. As a young teenager, Thea's whole life was centered on avoiding starvation. It is no wonder Thea did not have a pattern inside her indicating how to be the mother of infants or adolescents. She hadn't experienced enmeshment with her mother as an infant. In war-torn France normal adolescent individuation was impossible.

Thea was a survivor. Her characterological structure focused on staying alive and appreciating pleasures. It was mystifying to her that her children seemed to take being alive so lightly. Their lack of appreciation for comforts and opportunities infuriated her, though she denied the rage.

Her grandchild was the lever which forced Thea to modify her behavior. Michelle's bulimia and Renee's drug use were not sufficient motivations. Michelle very much wanted her mother to share in the excitement of pregnancy and infant care. However, she discovered, as she matured in therapy, that she could not tolerate being patronized any more. Advice and criticism made her sick. Thea changed, protesting all the way. The reward was a much richer relationship with Michelle and Renee.

If Thea had not been so sure she was right about everything, I would not have had to protect Michelle and the infant so directly. Shannon has ninety years to live. As a society, we must try to give her as good a start as possible. A calm, cheerful, ever-present mother is a prerequisite for adult mental health. Americans are more anxious than people from Africa, the Orient, India, or South America. I believe that is because we have lost the art of mothering. Michelle was eager to learn how to be a good mother. She had to be protected from external stress while Shannon was tiny.

God's Strange Ways

Thea took to the recollection of Scripture with her characteristic energetic enthusiasm. She loved to learn; exploring new concepts was a delight. Her spiritual director guided her reading, highlighting the main points and keeping her on track. She devoured the lives of saints, past and present.

Thea realized her childish picture of Santa Claus in the sky refusing to return her beloved father because he was mean, was not an accurate representation of the Almighty. God sustained her mother through evil days brought on by man's disobedience, as He sustained Jesus through the cross. Her daily prayer life and Bible reading became her most cherished times. Soon the whole family became involved, joining a church and praying together. Our God uses strange ways of drawing people to Himself. To Him be the glory.

"That they all may be one; as thou, Father, art in me, and I in thee, that they also may be one in us: that the world may believe that thou has sent me" (John 17:21 KJV).

8
Find a New Way of Being

RAY

Synopsis: Ray and his wife, Marge, had been devoted to the Lord all their lives. Their pastors suggested that steadfastness in daily prayer, reading of the Word, tithing, and church involvement would result in marital harmony and successful children. Ray became very depressed when his youngsters got into trouble. We resolved that crisis but three years later his wife asked him to move out. Ray became disoriented and extremely anxious away from his family. Instead of living alone, nursing his grievances, Ray decided to be a house parent in a home for disturbed youngsters. By giving them counsel and hope, he was transformed. Therapy allowed Ray to renew his covenanted relationship with Marge. God created in them "a pure heart" and renewed "a steadfast spirit" (Psalm 51:10).

Find a New Way of Being

I first met Ray and Marge to discuss their son's academic difficulties. Despite above average academic competence, Stan was flunking out of his senior year in high school. He refused to study, missed classes, and had disappeared for several days at a time. At home he was rude to his parents and mean to his little sister. Carol wasn't doing very well in the ninth grade either. She thought about clothes and boys exclusively it seemed. Ray and Marge were baffled as to why their children were turning out so badly. They had both spent a great deal of time with them. They attended church regularly; the youngsters belonged to choir and youth groups. It was a puzzlement!

Ray and Marge were attractive people in their early forties. He was a dentist. She went to work as an executive secretary in a medical firm after their daughter entered kindergarten. They both came from solid families of Scottish extraction. Her parents were farmers. His father was a grocer in Kansas. After the Second World War, they bought their present home in California.

I hear this story over and over. Difficulties occur with the children even though the parents have conscientiously tried to do everything correctly. They had been to all the teachers' meetings, supervised homework, and made strict rules on the advice of a school psychologist, all to no avail. Both youngsters continued to act out. Stan wouldn't come home when he was told. Carol didn't help around the house. Stan was messy. Carol dressed very peculiarly, etcetera, etcetera and so forth.

Blaming Each Other

The second time we talked together, I began to see that each parent was blaming the other. The father thought that the mother was too lenient; the mother thought that the father was too strict. They disagreed about money. Marge believed the children should be given money for various activities. Ray believed they should earn it. They disagreed about recreation time. She believed the family should spend a lot of time together going places and doing things. He wanted to have his beloved wife to himself, on occasions.

Ray agreed Marge was a caring mother, but felt she was overly attentive to the children's desires and overly forgiving when they broke the rules. Marge thought Ray was stern and unsympathetic. He didn't really understand the difficulties of being a teenager in today's world. They also disagreed about Marge's mother. Marge said the church taught she should see her mother every day, as the old lady was a widow with severe arthritis and failing eyesight. Ray believed she was spending far too much time attending to her mother.

I was able to help them be firm with Stan. They decided he could not live at home anymore if he didn't go to school regularly and maintain C grades. I told Ray there were seven things that he and Marge should say to Stan and Carol every day and nothing else:

"Good morning."

"You look terrific!"

"Hope you have a good day."

"Here's a delicious breakfast for you."

"Dinner time."

"Hope you sleep well."

"Good night, my love."

They asked, "How will we get the chores done?"

"Write a note; stick it on the refrigerator listing all the chores you expect Stan and Carol to do each week. Allow them to decide when to do them."

"How can we be sure the dog gets fed?"

"If the dog isn't fed, take it to the pound unless you want to feed it."

"How can we get their rooms tidied up?"

"If anything is out of place on Monday, hide it. Otherwise, ignore them."

Ray and Marge went home from that session and spelled out the new rules. The steady stream of criticism and advice stopped. Stan pulled himself together, worked very hard, and finished high school with a B- average. Carol took responsibility for her own schoolwork, limiting her social life voluntarily.

During further sessions, we rejoiced at the new tranquillity and refined their reactions to annoying behavior. I spent a great deal of time encouraging Ray and Marge to trust their kids, urging them to start enjoying each other instead of worrying about Stan and Carol. I suggested they not talk about their youngsters at all, writing notes to each other if decisions had to be made. After several months their home had settled down so they decided to discontinue therapy.

Another Tragedy

Three years later Ray called saying he needed to see me. I asked about the children and he reported they were doing very well in college. I was delighted. We set an appointment for the next week.

When he came in, Ray looked haggard and exhausted. A tall man, muscular from daily exercise, he was normally at the peak of health.

I asked, "What has happened?"

"My wife asked me to move out. We began to argue a lot. Then she stopped wanting to make love. It's been hell."

This tragedy often happens. In systems theory, we know that when people change, stresses and strains appear in other parts of the family. Until my previous intervention, the children had been the problems. Husband and wife were drawn together to help them. Daily conversations revolved around the latest misdemeanor, debating what they were going to do. When I forbade that kind of dialogue, encouraging them to begin enjoying each other, trouble started. The children ceased being the identified problems, the bad guys, and the parents discovered their interpersonal difficulties.

Ray explained, "There was more and more tension. Our sex life became almost nonexistent. I couldn't say anything without Marge yelling or crying. I don't know what's going on. Perhaps it's her menopause. It has been very uncomfortable around our home. She always talked about how her feelings were hurt because I didn't understand her or really care about the family. That's not true. I don't know what I did wrong. Last week Marge asked me to move out. She said she had been angry since the beginning of our marriage; she never really loved me. That hurts. She needs to get away from me to actualize herself. I don't know what to do."

Ray was in real psychological danger. His identity was as Marge's husband and the children's father, the supporter of the family. The home, where he had spent many long hours fixing things, was his haven, his place of relaxation. Banned from the house, he was confused and anxious. In his small apartment he couldn't relax enough to cook, read, or watch television. Ray ate junk food, pacing about his apartment. Every night by three in the morning he was wide awake, having slept only a few hours.

You're Poisoning Yourself

Ray was seriously depressed. Every line in his body telegraphed unhappiness and abandonment. He told me at length about each situation where there had been a misunderstanding. He recited what she had said and what he had said and what other people had said. After two hours of listening, I finally remarked, "You'll get sick if you keep these thoughts going round and round in your mind."

"I know. It's awful. I can't stop thinking about my wife and the things we said to each other."

"The Bible tells us we have to forgive and go forward."

Angrily he replied, "That's easy to say but very difficult to do."

Calmly, "I know. I know. But you're poisoning yourself. I believe you'll be talking again within six months. In the meantime you need to stay steady, using this time to grow in your relationship with Christ."

"I know but it's lonely; I'm restless living by myself."

"Well, then, move in with my friend who runs a shelter for disturbed adolescents. They need another strong man around. You'd be able to teach them about the Lord."

His eyes brightened. "Would that be possible? I'd love to talk with those youngsters. Could I really be used to encourage them?"

"Of course. After work every day, you can go home to needy kids to play ball, eat dinner, hang out. On weekends you can teach them to ski, your favorite sport. They need your wisdom and counsel." Ray moved in the next week and enjoyed his time with the teenagers.

Marge wanted her freedom, and found Ray restrictive and unempathic. She wasn't interested in joint counseling about their marriage. She longed to discover her real self. Insisting she come in for weekly counseling on communication styles or family games was pointless. I knew that once the first flush of freedom wore off, Marge would begin to miss Ray's companionship. Because of the intricate interweaving of their lives for twenty-three years with friends, church, and children, separation would begin to feel like amputation.

My main fear was that another woman would come along and get her hooks into Ray before Marge had time to experience the loss. Though his depression would lift rapidly through pleasure in being admired, his mixed loyalties could be very hard to reconcile. Christians know marriage is a covenanted relationship. Given time, God always works on each heart for reconciliation. I discerned that they would come to their senses. In the meantime, Ray needed protection from predatory women looking for a handsome, gentle man. In therapy we worked on learning to enjoy blessed singleness.

Standing Alone

Our Lord tells us that each man must learn to stand by himself. He made Peter leave his fishing and his wife, which gave his mother-in-law the vapors (Matthew 8:14). She was appalled that her son-in-law would follow a traveling teacher rather than support her and produce grandchildren as was customary in Israel. Jesus' willingness to separate spouses was hard to understand. "And everyone who has left houses or brothers or sisters or father or mother or wife or children or fields for my sake will receive a hundred times as much and will inherit eternal life" (Matthew 19:29).

In today's world being paired is more important than commitment to the living God. We are bombarded daily through the media with the idea that all single people yearn to be joined to somebody else. The old-fashioned concepts of blessed singleness and the joys of celibacy are considered foolish. It is a popular notion that one's mate is one's best friend; that a person can share anything with his significant other. Sex is the supreme event, signifying emotional and physical union.

Scripture indicates that the passionate, all-consuming involvement of the major figures in the Bible is their relationship with
God. Some of them were married: Abraham, Isaac, Jacob, Moses,
and Peter. But Jesus wasn't married and He didn't encourage His
disciples to get married. He never said to any of His disciples,
"Why don't you get engaged to that nice woman over there? You
should have a family." He never said, "The family that prays together, stays together." Nor did He give insights into child rearing.

Of course, He honored marriage and forbade divorce. A stable,
affectionate relationship between two people is the proper nurturing ground for children. An infant's long immaturity makes it
very difficult for one person to meet all his emotional and physical needs. Single parenting can be done, as tragically we're seeing
in the 1980s in America, where many youngsters are being raised
by one adult. But it certainly is not optimal. A child needs both a
mother and a father, and, of course, Jesus knew that. But the
raising of children wasn't a priority for the One who came to
teach kingdom living.

For centuries religious families gave their best, the strongest,
brightest, and most creative child, to the church, and their second
most capable son to support the country. Their third son devoted
himself to business and supporting all the indigent relatives, carrying on the family lineage through children. A son or daughter
dedicated to God, offering a lifetime of praise and service, was
considered the highest good.

A mother was honored by her whole village if her child took
holy orders. No need for grandchildren here; no sentimental
Hallmark cards about grandmother were desired. Service of God
was the most important calling. He was the One a person talked
to when depressed and turned to for comfort in grief. God was
the best companion in times of trouble and in times of joy, in
times of celebration and in times of working.

This seems to be closer to Jesus' thinking than does the modern
cult of finding a significant other, of having one's children take care
of one's emotional needs, or worshiping grandchildren. Jesus came
to tell us to walk the path rejoicing in the presence of God, talking

with Him, laughing with Him, weeping with Him. If you live that way, then you are not seduced by money or power or sexual attractions, nor dismayed by the disappointments and losses of this life. They are all relative; only God is absolute. As Kierkegaard said, "Render unto the relative, relatively, and unto the absolute, absolutely." Jesus came to bring us the peace that passes understanding. Common sense doesn't understand how somebody can be peaceful in the midst of triumph and tragedy. But Christians know that life is a training school for our souls, a journey designed with mountains to climb, rivers to cross, and losses to endure. Joy comes in the midst of difficulties if our eyes are fixed on Christ.

Ray was an enormous blessing to the young people. He counseled and played handball. As a good, strong man who loved the Lord passionately, he was the best possible witness for the disturbed kids with whom he lived.

Ray's depression lifted as he plunged into interacting. Ray was sad not to be with his wife and children, but he wasn't frantic anymore. He learned to enjoy his time alone, communing intimately with God. He no longer needed other people.

Love without Need

After six months, Ray said, "My wife called and she wants me to come to dinner."

I exclaimed, "Wonderful! What fun!"

Suspiciously, "How should I handle it? I bet she wants money."

"Very carefully. Tell her that you love her and want to be with her. Do not bring up old resentments, gripes, and irritations."

Ray asked, "How will she know to stop doing all those distressing things?"

"She won't. But you've changed, and you'll find they don't bother you so much. You've mellowed, living with all those disturbed teenagers. You're not nearly as judgmental and rigid."

"You taught me to appreciate, admire, listen to, and enjoy the kids. Should I be with Marge the same way?"

"Yes; that's agape love, love without need."

"Okay," he remarked. "I'll try it." And so he did.

At our next session Ray looked radiant. He had increased his empathic listening skills attending to the young people. It was easy to take pleasure in his wife's recounting of various activities that she was enjoying. He liked looking at her, laughing with her, and using the "in" language they had developed during their marriage. When she brought up certain problems with the children that began to push his buttons, he remembered not to react. Smiling sweetly, he'd ask, "Tell me how you feel about it. What do you think we ought to do?"

The reason Marge asked him to dinner was, indeed, to discuss money. Ray was very conservative when it came to dollars; he was a penny pincher. He wanted to save his substantial income for the education of his children and retirement. He had no interest in consumer goods. His wife, on the other hand, liked to keep a nice house and buy fashionable clothes. Money had always been a bone of contention between them. When finances came up at their reunion, Ray gripped the bottom of his chair to hold himself quiet. He listened calmly. When she asked for his opinion, he followed my instructions carefully. "My darling, I'll have to think about it. I don't know exactly what I want to do. Let me pray for twenty-four hours and I'll get back to you." She was visibly relieved that he hadn't become angry. They parted filled with new hope. Ray was elated because the evening had been enormously successful.

They continued to meet once a week for the next three months. He wouldn't fight. Every time she brought up an issue on which he had a strong opinion, he held his tongue. When she pressed him for an answer, he would say, "I have to pray about that."

Three months later Ray told me that Marge wanted to come to a session. I replied, "Fine, as long as you come, too." When they both came to my office, I was delighted to see her.

She said, "I am bewildered. I can't quite figure out whether this new behavior is for real. Will Ray continue to be able to listen without getting angry or is it some trick that you taught him to get back in my good graces?"

She talked at length about how she had agonized over asking him to move out. She loved him very much but found his rigid opinions and miserliness more than she could bear. He would storm around the house pointing out the sins and wickednesses of the children, neighbors, church people, and his office personnel.

"Since we have gotten back together again for dinner, Ray appears to be calm and cheerful. I know he doesn't always agree with me as to how to handle situations or money, but he doesn't lecture and make me feel like an ignoramus. I asked to see you because I want to know if this is going to last or will Ray become his old self when we move back together again?"

Miracles Sometimes Take Trauma

There were a number of different ways to answer. I could have replied, "You two will need a lot of marital counseling, communication training, and sexual therapy. We must explore unconscious conflicts so that you don't regress into bad patterns." Or, "If I were you, I'd be very careful because you can't teach an old dog new tricks. He'll probably revert when he's safely back in his own home."

I could have drawn up a behavioral program or tried to adjudicate their problems. I might have explained the games they played or their family systems.

Instead, God brought Joseph to my mind. So I talked about that very opinionated, self-righteous young man. The biblical narrative describes his flaunting the many-colored coat and his dreams about cattle and corn. Ray and Joseph had characteristics in common; they believed they were right until God humbled them.

God often allows a traumatic happening to produce change. In Joseph's case, after being sold into slavery in Egypt, he was jailed on false charges; in Ray's, it was being told by his beloved wife that he had to leave his home and family. God transformed both men from the inside out. They could not revert to their old arrogance. Ray's prayer over these long months to have the mind of Christ, had been granted. "You can take him back with joy," I replied.

At home, Ray demonstrated a quiet humor, and an unwillingness to get drawn into arguments. Marge also changed. Issues which had seemed important faded in the harmony of their home. The effect on the children was dramatic. Instead of avoiding their parents, they began to come home from college for weekends to talk. They sought Ray's counsel, finding him available and wise. Marge delighted in their relationships and enjoyed the family get-togethers. The last I heard they were giving God the glory for their transformed lives.

Ray

Conclusion: God's healing power creates miracles. "Seek first His Kingdom and His righteousness, and all these things will be given to you as well" (Matthew 6:33). Ray's psyche was soaked in the Word; he had listened and read all his life. Despite difficulties in his childhood, which led to miserliness and rigidity, Ray yearned to have the mind of Christ.

He was not aware of his characterological disorder; it's very hard to know ourselves. For God to continue Ray's sanctification, Marge's heart was turned against him. His judgments and penny pinching were the reasons given, but I suspect she lost her enthusiasm for being in his company. Little things he did annoyed her; mannerisms evoked rage. Marge never intended to feel irritable toward Ray. She began to feel suffocated in their relationship. I believe God arranged these occurrences so that they could "become mature, attaining to the whole measure of the fullness of Christ" (Ephesians 4:13).

They both grew up. With Ray gone from the house, Marge was able to experience herself and sort out her internal feelings from her reactions to Ray. She became more open to him, able to forgive as the weeks lengthened into months. Ray's rigid beliefs had been jolted repeatedly, living with disturbed young adults. As he listened to them talk, trying to provide help and comfort, his life with Marge looked very blessed in hindsight. He empathized with his own children, realizing they had been through identity crises he hadn't understood at the time.

As a result of insights gained in therapy, Ray became less authoritarian. Initially, he was a poor candidate for counseling because he didn't think anything was wrong with him. He knew right from wrong and believed a man should teach his family. It was good stewardship to be very careful with money. I could have told him in our first session that he needed more empathy for others' opinions, but he wouldn't have been able to make that insight operational in his life. God provided the young adults for his growth. They shared themselves with him and he grew to love those very unlike himself. Ray's giving of himself, instead of obsessing about Marge's unfairness, provided the plowed field into which seeds of self-knowledge could be sown in therapy.

Becoming Citizens of the Kingdom

The infinite variety of human experiences is God's way of making us citizens of the kingdom. To transform us into disciples, we have to be derailed from our habitual ways of being. Peter, Andrew, James, and John gave up their nets to beg for daily bread. Mr. and Mrs. Zebedee lost the earning power of their strong sons in a day when sons were the only social security and retirement plan. Saul lost his political influence, his rabbinical prestige, and his capacity to earn enough to live a comfortable life when he became the apostle Paul. At his brain power level, with his advanced degrees, tent making was a real occupational comedown. He didn't come from a family of tent makers; he never envisioned he'd work with his hands. New wine is not put in old wineskins (Matthew 9:17).

Off-track Lives

I am always amazed that Christians are so surprised when their lives go off-track. Jesus began His ministry by leaving Nazareth. His mother needed His carpentry to support the younger children; she needed His emotional help to raise the four little kids. His high school friends, the boys He coached in ball games, the students He taught at the synagogue, the old ladies He helped with chores around their homes—all of them depended on Him. He just walked away. People say, "But He was God." Of course, He was God. He took on human flesh and became a man to show us how to live. "He was in the world, and though the world was made through Him, the world did not recognize Him" (John 1:10–11), because its people were too stuck on their familiar tracks.

"The world is too much with us late and soon/ Getting and spending we lay waste our powers. Little we know of nature that is ours." In this poem, nature means God's creation. Wordsworth goes on to say, "Oh God, I'd rather be a pagan suckled on a creed outworn/ so might I, standing on this pleasant lea, have glimpses that would make me less forlorn."

Forlorn we are in this age of anxiety. We cannot see God's hand molding us into appropriate vessels for His Holy Spirit. "We are poor little lambs who have lost our way, baa, baa, baa. We are poor little sheep who have gone astray, baa, baa, baa . . . God have mercy on such as we, baa, baa, baa!" (*Whiffenpoof song*, Yale University)

What is "the poor little lambs'" way? Jesus is the "way, the truth, and the life" (John 14:6). What is the plan of creation? Jesus came to show us how to live. If His life jumped out of habitual tracks, why are we so surprised when our lives are turned upside down?

Unfortunately, comfort and predictability have been promised to faithful churchgoers, instead of the pilgrim's way that ends with a cross. Health and wealth, prosperity theology, leads to damnation. Apostate churches prioritize social activities and good deeds, forgetting that Jesus said our main concern must be a right relationship with God. Works flow out of transformed lives filled with the Holy Spirit.

"Therefore if any man be in Christ, he is a new creature: old things are passed away; behold, all things are become new" (2 Corinthians 5:17 KJV).

9

You Want to Kill Your Mother

FRANCIE

Synopsis: Overweight, heavily medicated, and bitter, Francie came into therapy reluctantly, having experienced many past failures trying to get psychological help. She had been obsessed with fears since the birth of her first child nine years previously. Her supportive husband and two sons desperately wanted her to find relief. A long-term, twice-a-week therapy produced a solid transference relationship, allowing her unconscious to divulge its secrets. A dream set her free to be the slim, vivacious, charming woman Francie is today. Her gratitude to God for this miracle after years of suffering has brought her into church as a new Christian.

You Want to Kill Your Mother

When I met Francie, she was about thirty pounds overweight, with mousy brown hair, no makeup, wearing clothes that indicated she felt badly about her body. She said that her mind was filled with terror much of the time; she was afraid snakes were going to strike her children. She would startle awake at night, frightened that the boys had been struck and not told her. When they went out of the house to school, she was frightened that snakes would come down on the playground. On bad days, she would ask them twenty-five or thirty times whether they had seen a snake.

The boys, Tommy and Mark, were tired of the question. They were nine and eleven years old. They had heard it so many hundreds of times, they responded with exasperation. Even worse for Francie, sometimes they didn't respond at all, shrugging their shoulders and teasing her with a noncommittal, "Maybe I have and maybe I haven't." It drove Francie into a further frenzy of anxiety. She would beg them to tell her if they had seen any snakes, touched any snakes, been struck by any snakes.

Francie was on heavy medication. Psychiatrists had prescribed an antipsychotic which kept her feeling dull and drowsy all day. Furthermore, it made her gain weight.

She hated to be fat. She had always had a very trim, attractive figure as a girl, with a very small waist. It was excruciating for her to inhabit an out-of-shape body; she saw herself as gross.

Francie's husband, Richard, was very solicitous about Francie's condition. He tried to reassure her that the boys were all right. He helped her with the housework. They did many family activities together, particularly fishing.

Francie and Richard would pack up the children, go into the mountains, and catch trout all weekend. Richard was a big help on these trips, packing the car, fixing the meals, baiting the hooks, and staying very cheerful. Interestingly enough, Francie did not fear snakes in the mountains, where presumably there were more snakes than in the city.

At home Francie got up three or four times every night to check the locks. She was not afraid that burglars would come in, although her husband worked nights and she was alone with the children. She was afraid that the boys would go out and be struck by a snake during the night. Sometimes she would put a strip of tape over the door so that she could be sure they hadn't gone outdoors.

Neurotic — but Brave

Other than her extreme obsession about snakes striking her children, Francie was a very brave woman. She had traveled back and forth across the country several times with her toddlers, following her husband to different jobs. She had no fear of camping or of wild animals in the mountains. Ever since she was a little girl, she had been superb with horses. Somehow she knew exactly what they were thinking, and could gentle and tame the most difficult animal. People marveled at her skill. Furthermore, she enjoyed it. She loved to take on a cantankerous, angry, frustrated animal and turn him into a lovely pleasure horse.

I asked Francie about her relationship with her husband and she said it was excellent. She said they really got along well, enjoyed each other, and worked hard to raise the children and put aside some money. They owned a nice house with a swimming pool in a beautiful part of the city and a mountain cabin where they often went on weekends.

I asked Francie about her early life; she replied it had been very difficult. Her mother was a nervous woman. She spent hours every day talking to her mother, Francie's grandmother, on the phone or in person, because her grandparents lived next door. The gist of those conversations was her mother's frustration with life. Everything bothered her. Everything Francie did bothered her. Everything her husband did bothered her. Everything that happened outside her home upset her, and most everything that happened inside the home bothered her too. She was a woman driven by her own fears and paranoid projections. Francie was continuously told by her mother not to upset her, to behave, to do what she was told without asking any questions.

Francie's reaction to this when she was a little girl was to be very naughty. She remembers once going to a neighbor's house, and while the grownups were talking, taking maple syrup and squirting it all over the living room furniture. Another time, when she was about four, she took her grandmother's little dog and threw it off the balcony. This kind of acting out in an intelligent little girl suggests that she was living under too much stress and didn't have any legitimate way to express it.

Francie's father seems to have been largely absent, emotionally, if not physically. He came home every evening and hid in front of the television, or behind his newspaper, going to bed early and rising at dawn for another long day of work. His way of dealing with a continually upset woman was not to pay attention. Francie didn't have any brothers or sisters. Her grandmother was dedicated to trying to soothe her distraught daughter. She wasn't a comfort to her granddaughter.

Francie had a wonderful relationship with her grandfather; they were almost inseparable. Whenever she could, she spent time sitting on his lap, listening to his stories, and playing games with him. Suddenly when she was six, he wouldn't spend any more time with her. It was the most bitter blow of her life. To this day she doesn't know what happened. Perhaps her mother got jealous of their relationship. Perhaps her grandmother called him a dirty old man and suggested something sexual was going on. From that day on, her grandfather avoided her like the plague. The effect of that abandonment shocked Francie into being good. For the next fourteen years, until she left home, Francie tried in every way she could to help her mother stay calm. She was a dutiful little girl, and a quiet teenager. The acting out behavior stopped. She began to live internally in a fantasy world.

Francie did very well in school, though she never felt close to any friends. She was attractive and people enjoyed being with her. Her internal world was more real than the external one. She covered this preference for the inner world by cheerfully going about her daily tasks, making very good grades in school, and to all outward appearances, being a normal child. However, when I asked Francie the names of some of her friends in junior high and high school, she couldn't remember. She never spent the night at another child's home, nor did she invite children to her home for birthday parties, or an afternoon of play, as it would upset her mother. She wandered lonely as a cloud through school, and dutifully did her housework and homework every evening.

When she was fourteen, Francie acquired a horse. Now her world revolved around the stable; she lived and breathed for Sandy. By spending all her free time with her horse, she became very aware of how Sandy felt and thought. Being strong and athletic, it was easy for her to become a superior rider. Other people in the stable asked for help with their horses' peculiarities and she enjoyed thinking of ways to help horses break bad habits. After a couple of years, she could ride any horse in the stable, even the most difficult. Her balance was superb, her hands were light, and she could anticipate what the horse was going to do. Her mother liked horses, though she was never a rider. She would come out occasionally and watch Francie riding.

Nine Years of Terror

At twenty Francie met Richard and during the next year they happily rode together on the trails. Richard was a good rider, though not as gifted as Francie. He loved to get out into the countryside. When he proposed to her, she accepted gladly. Richard had to go back east for a couple of years to work so she had to sell Sandy. It was traumatic parting from her horse, but she felt ready for the new adventure of marriage and looked forward to living in another part of the country.

A month after she was married, they moved east. The next month her mother committed suicide. Though shocked, Francie maintained her composure, flew home to the funeral, comforted grieving relatives, and flew back to join her husband. She didn't take much time off from her demanding job as a clothes buyer for a large department store. To all outward appearances, Francie managed the loss of the horse, the new living environment, and the death of her mother smoothly and well. Not until the birth of her first child did she become obsessional.

When Mark was two months old, Richard had to go on a three-week business trip. Francie began to lose it. Being cooped up all day with a crying infant without anyone to help her learn the rudiments of infant care, and without friends (because all the people she knew were working), Francie began to be very anxious. At first, it was just free-floating anxiety. She felt nervous all the time. Slowly it increased to the point that she became agoraphobic. She had real difficulties going outside the house, even though she couldn't pinpoint what it was that frightened her.

Richard was very solicitous. He took her to a doctor who prescribed antianxiety medication. He relieved her of some of the stress of infant care by managing Mark after work and on weekends.

Francie continued to wrestle with fear. She had been in and out of doctors' and psychologists' offices for eleven years. Her obsessions changed; only recently had she become afraid of snakes. But the patterns of obsessive thoughts, terrorizing her, never completely disappeared.

Being a psychologist is like being a detective, a Sherlock Holmes of human behavior. I asked her about the many treatment modalities that other therapists tried. It seemed to Francie that she had talked endlessly to well-meaning counselors about her fears. She remained very frightened. A variety of medications from the mildest sedatives to the anti-psychotics had been prescribed. They made her feel stupid and tired. Worst of all, she always gained weight.

There was no point in seeing this as a family system's problem. By self-report, which I confirmed after I spent an hour with Richard, their family life was good. The boys were stars, bright and creative. They were doing well in school, enjoyed their friends, and played Little League baseball every week. They adapted to their mother's peculiarities. She had been a superb infant mother enjoying nursing, holding, rocking, and caring for each child when they were tiny. Her agoraphobia served to keep her more available for them.

In some tribes in Africa, young women with new babies are housed in a separate section of the village. All they do is play with their infants for twenty-four months and talk with the other mothers. They are relieved of all food-gathering chores and ceremonial duties in the tribe. These highly sophisticated natives understand how crucial it is that a mother's attention be primarily focused on her infant for the first two years of its life. The young women of those tribes are not even expected to be available to their husbands sexually, though they can choose to spend time together. All she has to do all day, every day, is watch, nurse, walk, play with, and sleep with her baby.

Francie had done that with her infants. Her husband was her best friend and they enjoyed each other; he was all the adult company she wanted. She felt fulfilled. The little boys reflected that devotion. They were developmentally superior, intellectually gifted, and very charming.

The likelihood of behavior modification techniques working in as long-standing an obsessional pattern as Francie presented was very slim. I couldn't argue her out of her obsession using rational-emotive techniques. If I used the Gestalt chair technique, and split her between the part of herself that was obsessional and the part of herself that knew better, she could have a delightful dialogue because both Francies were available. I do not mean to suggest that she was a multiple personality; she just knew how silly it was to worry about snakes. As Carl Rogers suggests, for several months I gave her perfect freedom to share all she was thinking. But the obsession continued. I was left, therefore, with only one alternative. I had to reach Junior and try to persuade the little one inside not to be so afraid. The therapeutic modality of choice was long-term, dynamic, supportive dreamwork.

Junior is accurately reached through dreams. Twice a week, she brought her dreams and we analyzed them. After Francie told me a dream, I would say, "What are your associations?" since the manifest content of the dream has very little significance. There are dream books on the market purporting to say what water or fire or fuzzy animals or automobiles mean in dreams. Though symbols seem to have similar significance some of the time, each dream must be analyzed from the associations made to the manifest content, that is, the remembered story. Most importantly, I wanted to know how she felt in the dream. As a therapist, I had to be terribly careful not to put my own associations into the interpretation of her dreams, at least until we worked together long enough so that our unconscious minds resonated together, creating a therapeutic alliance.

Murderous Dreams

After about a year of working together, Francie came in with two dreams one week. In both of them she had tried to strangle her sons. Horrified, she asked, "Do you think I really want to kill my youngsters?"

I assured her, "Manifest content isn't the message. There is not a chance you are talking about killing your boys, though on occasion all mothers can get very irritated with their kids. Strangling stops the nagging and whining. Your boys don't nag or whine. Is there anybody you wanted to stop having to hear, someone who nagged and whined and filled the air with her complaints?"

After a long pause, Francie said, "I remember my mother used to pick up snakes all the time. My father once said that she'd better be careful or a poisonous snake would strike and she'd die."

"Have you ever consciously thought about wanting your mother to die?"

Indignantly, "Absolutely not! I felt very sorry for her."

I suggested, "Perhaps Junior Francie wanted her mother to die and hoped the snakes would do her in."

For a youngster who hopes, albeit unconsciously, that her mother will die, if mother does die prematurely, she believes she made it happen. Now, of course, to our logical, rational brains, it is perfectly clear that Francie was married and in another part of the country when her mother took her own life. But the unconscious doesn't think that way. You will remember, it is only two years old. And two-year-olds are great magic workers. Having not yet discovered the laws of the natural world, they really believe that if they think certain things, or move their hands in certain ways, or step on cracks in the sidewalk, or forget to say their prayers at night, they will cause bad things to happen. Francie's adult self knew she hadn't caused her mother to die; but the child inside Francie felt that somehow or other, by magic, she had arranged her mother's death. Junior began to punish her, first with free-floating anxiety and, later on, with obsessional fears.

Heartbreaking Coverup

Francie's children resembled her mother in some ways. She had a strong desire to care for them, even though sometimes they were demanding and irritating. They dominated her world; she could never get away from their needs and feelings. Her husband was her companion, but her children were the center of her emotional life. It was simple, unconsciously, to slide the children into her mother's slot. They became the objects of obsessions which covered her terror that, somehow or other, she would injure them. Like all two-year-olds, Francie's Junior had two competing thoughts. One was to get rid of the mother who was consuming and irritating; the other was to keep her alive for needed nurture.

At Children's Hospital, Los Angeles, where I interned for two years, it was heartbreaking to counsel kids who had been severely abused by their parents, physically or sexually. One little girl, who had both of her arms broken by her mother, was seen for the third time in the emergency room. We placed her in a comfortable foster home. She begged me, weekly, to let her go back to her family. She said, "It was my fault that my mom broke my arms and put out cigarettes on my back. I was supposed to have supervised my baby brother and kept him from crying. I know my mother is nervous. When mom gets upset, she does things she doesn't mean to do. Please let me go home to help my mom." All children raised by abusive parents have difficulty in rapprochement. They cannot get free from needed-hated mother because they are never given sufficient nurture to make them independent people.

Francie received sufficient nurture from me in our therapeutic alliance to feel like an independent person. I mirrored her into maturity. Following those dreams, the obsession waned. She kept saying, nervously, "Some other fear will begin to control my mind." But it didn't happen. Instead, she went off the medication under doctor's care and began to lose weight. Her energy returned; a sparkle appeared in her eyes. She landed a job as a salesperson for a pharmaceutical company, making cold calls on doctors all day long. To me, the thought of walking in, unexpected, unannounced, to a busy doctor's office to talk him into buying something he didn't particularly want is even more frightening than training wild horses! For her, it was easy and she was successful. Francie began to make sales in a very difficult territory within her first month on the job.

Once she had earned a little money, Francie bought a very green quarter horse. Day after day Francie stood in a dusty paddock after work, lunging her horse while her boys took lessons nearby. After three months, she put a saddle on his back and rode with the boys. Francie had the great pleasure of knowing herself to be a highly skillful horse trainer once again.

The therapeutic breakthrough came when Francie realized she had wanted to kill her mother. She learned that her rage at her mother had gone underground at six; her extremely compliant childhood and adolescence covered an interior ferment. It was possible for her to own her murderous rage when she realized that this was how Junior felt; the adult person wasn't a murderer. The feelings repressed into her unconscious surfaced when her first child was born because she felt responsible for her mother's death. She was afraid her magic would kill the baby.

Francie was awed by the power of the unconscious to affect behavior, attitudes, feelings, the very quality of life itself. Counselors had told her for years to pull herself together and stop being phobic, paranoid, obsessional. Until she and I developed a close enough working relationship so that her Junior could trust us with the secret of her murderous rage against her mother, Francie couldn't manage her own life. When she discovered her rage at her mother and the irrational fear that she had caused her death, Francie was set free.

Francie

Conclusions: Most therapists try the obvious and easiest therapeutic modalities first. Behavior modification, or cognitive behavior modification, changes situations quickly if it is going to work at all. In Francie's case that would mean saying something like this: "Count the number of times you think about snakes striking your children each day for a week. Once we've established a baseline, the average number of thoughts per day, then we can plan another thought or action to block the obsession. The new thought or action will ultimately replace your fear about snakes." Under the guidance of previous psychologists, Francie had already tried to control her thoughts. A new fear would replace the original fear in a matter of months.

Talking in a safe atmosphere sometimes helps. Carl Rogers evolved client-centered therapy to help people get in touch with themselves. They could discover their deepest feelings and make more appropriate decisions in life. Interpersonal relationships improved and quality-of-life quotients rose significantly.

Francie had tried Rogerian therapy. She was charming and articulate; therapists liked her. The only problem was she didn't recover. Her phobias and obsessions continued to plague her because she didn't have access to her unconscious feelings.

Many clients can go through the repression barrier to experience their unconscious conflicts. In Francie's case, however, the unconscious needed her to stay phobic and hypervigilant. All the best efforts of counselors had been thwarted by Junior. Her unconscious belief was that if she gave up the defense of phobic terrors, her children would die. She needed to stay alert and frightened so her magic wouldn't escape to kill her children, because she believed she'd killed her mother.

I carefully analyzed the family system, discovering that Richard liked the role of caretaker. I hypothesized that he grew up caring for his mother, so his Junior was addicted to being a support. He confirmed my hypothesis when we talked. Even in high school he had sought out women who needed him. Francie and Richard's neurotic patterns locked together, reinforcing her sickness. Discussion of communication styles, interactive nonverbal messages, triangulation, games people play, or enhancing their sexual experiences would not have addressed the central presenting problem. Francie's fears and the disabling effects of the psychotropic medication were top priority. We would have to work on the marriage later on in therapy.

Explaining to Francie the unconscious dynamics causing her distress would not have been efficacious. Some understanding has to be shared to enhance trust in the therapist. However, rational-emotive insights will not remove terror from this kind of patient. No explanation could give her relief. Self-esteem exercises, assertion training, a primal scream experience, a growth group with loving supporters—none of these would reduce her anxiety.

Francie needed to get into an ongoing relationship with someone she could rely on. Because of her dysfunctional mother, she
would not be able to feel complete trust, but an intellectual belief
that I could help her made up for the underlying suspicion.

Trust is learned from trustworthy mothers; emotionally disturbed mothers produce youngsters who can never trust completely. Francie tested me every session. She would question what
I had said, my sanity, my feelings about her and my belief she
would recover. Through that year of visits and testing, her unconscious discovered, much to her surprise, that I really did care
about her adult self and Junior. I could be relied upon to listen
closely to her conscious and her unconscious. Despite herself,
Francie's little child took refuge.

Listening to Dreams

Dreams are fascinating! They speak in a language that has to be
learned, as does French or Chinese. Once learned, however, dream
language treats us to a voyage into buried material. Metaphor, symbols, reversals, and repetitions disguise the real (latent) content
from the conscious mind. Freud believed that Junior's thoughts
and feelings have to be disguised from the rational mind. The ego,
or conscious mind, doesn't approve of unconscious material; that's
why it is pushed below the repression barrier.

The first instruction always given to the client after a dream has
been recounted is to associate. That means to think about each
person, place, and thing in the dream, letting pictures and memories float to the surface. If the therapist sits quietly and waits,
Junior will provide the needed pieces to solve the riddle. In Francie's associations, the words her father spoke about snakes cleared
up the mystery. She'd had long practice in associating over the
months. At first, this process can be quite difficult for logical people, since dreams don't make rational sense.

Feelings in dreams and about dreams can also help with the
interpretation. It is very important to insist a patient like Francie
keep thinking about the dream, especially if she becomes uncomfortable. Phobias, after all, come from uncomfortable unconscious

conflicts. Her uneasiness signaled our approach to what Fritz Perls called a pain place. After all possible associations have been made and feelings explored, the dream has to be related to the day's residue, that is: whatever occurred on the day before the dream. It is worked through all night. Our previous learning is updated through dreams during "REM" sleep. The day's residue is integrated into the vast data bank of all past experiences. The computer in our heads is brought up-to-date daily through the software of dreams.

Having investigated the associations, feelings, and day's residue, and being knowledgeable about the patient's character structure, anxieties, chief defenses, and occurrences since the last visit, the therapist makes an interpretation. If it is accurate, the patient will feel an inner jolt of recognition. If it is not accurate, no damage is done unless the clinician frightens the client with unhelpful ideas, such as a suggestion that Francie wanted to kill her children. Even if an inaccurate interpretation is made, the patient works on the dream throughout the week, assuring Junior that someone is trying to understand the conflicts. That sense alone encourages the unconscious to keep trying to communicate.

God intends that each of us should grow into full maturity, wholeness, holiness. Our bodies, minds, and psyches want to evolve into their fullest potential. When I first met her, Francie couldn't trust God anymore than she could trust me. As we worked, the therapeutic miracle happened. She stopped obsessing, lost her phobias, got off medication, slimmed down, started training a young horse, and began a job. Years of hopelessness gave way to empowered living. The marriage of Francie and Richard survived the changes and blessed everyone who saw them together. They began attending church regularly, enrolled the children in Sunday school classes, and faithfully tithed in thanksgiving. As God raised Jesus from the dead, He gave new life to Francie. To Him be the glory! Amen.

"In the world ye shall have tribulation: but be of good cheer; I have overcome the world" (John 16:33 KJV).

10
Give Me Your Child

HEIDI

Synopsis: An addictive personality, Heidi, age twenty-two, had grown up without limits in a highly explosive atmosphere. When I threatened to take her young son away from her, she began long-term personality reconstruction psychotherapy. Because Heidi never learned how normal people function, much of our time was spent solving daily problems. Pregnancy with a second child gave us a drug-free period to discuss what really matters in life.

Give Me Your Child

Heidi was an addict. Her husband knew she used drugs heavily before they were married. She assured him she had given them up except for occasional recreational use. On Friday or Saturday nights, they both enjoyed a few lines of cocaine. He really didn't believe she was using regularly until he found the paraphernalia in the back of her closet. Steven was horrified. He didn't realize that she was addicted.

Heidi admitted that she used cocaine every day because she thought it made her a better mother. She found it boring to be with Samuel for long hours unless she was somewhat under the

117

influence. Nobody could tell because she'd used moderately for years. It was hard to sit still, much less concentrate on the babble of a two-and-a-half-year-old child. She liked the feeling using cocaine gave her.

I asked about her background. Heidi had never used alcohol, but she started using drugs when she was ten years old. By the time she was twelve, she had run away from home several times and, at thirteen, spent three months in a rehabilitation center. Her mother took a number of different pills; the bathroom cabinet looked like a pharmacy. Heidi had been jailed several times in her teens for shoplifting and running away. Every time her family tried to correct her she ran, sometimes not letting them know where she was for months.

Despite this confusion, Heidi graduated from high school. She then went to New England where she lived for two years in a Maine fishing village. She was very content; life was simple. She worked as a waitress in a local coffee shop and only used drugs occasionally. It was such a calming environment, she didn't feel the need of a daily dose. However, since Samuel's birth, Heidi had felt stressed out most of the time.

Childhood Chaos

I asked her what the emotional climate had been in her home as she was growing up. She grinned and said, "Very chaotic." Her mother and father fought all the time. There was yelling and slamming of doors. She couldn't count the number of times one or the other had marched out of the house saying they were never coming back. She didn't have any brothers or sisters to absorb this emotional abuse. As a little girl, she turned to an active fantasy life with imaginary playmates to comfort her when she was frightened. Every night she went to bed with all of her stuffed animals placed carefully, ritualistically around her bed to ward off any danger that might come in the night. I asked if she had ever been sexually abused and she said, "No." She had begun giving sexual favors to boys who would supply her with drugs when she was twelve, but she was never taken by force. She enjoyed sex because she liked being held and cuddled.

She met Steven when he visited her New England village to direct summer stock theater. They fell in love and were married in three months. She was nineteen, thoroughly delighted by his intelligence, good looks, and air of confidence. Steven was a very quiet man who worked long hours writing and producing plays. He used drugs recreationally but had no need for habitual consumption to calm inner nervousness. Proper mothering by a good farmer's wife in Wisconsin had given him serenity and safety. He seemed assured of becoming one of the great playwrights of our day.

You're Not Going to Take My Child Away

I said, "Heidi, you are abusing your child. Why don't you give him to me and then you can go on using drugs to your heart's content?"

She was shocked. "I wouldn't think of giving up Samuel! I adore Samuel."

"Fine, then you'll have to give up cocaine. But you can't have cocaine and Samuel. That's child abuse."

For a few moments she looked stunned. "You must be joking. You're not going to take my child away from me."

I replied, "I will if I can. You're abusing him, Heidi. He's an innocent victim. There's no way that Samuel can protect Samuel. Society, in the person of myself, is responsible for Samuel having a safe, secure, comfortable environment in which to learn and grow. You cannot provide that environment if you're using cocaine. You may think you look normal, but your true personality is being masked by the drug."

Indignantly Heidi replied, "I've been using it on a regular basis ever since I weaned him at nine months. Nobody has suggested that I was incompetent until now."

Steven exclaimed, "But you haven't been yourself, Heidi. While you were pregnant and nursing Samuel, you had a liveliness and a sense of humor that's almost disappeared. We'll have to find another way to help you manage internal anxiety."

Heidi was furious. "This is the stupidest discussion I've ever been in. This woman is crazy!" She jumped up and stalked out of the room. Steven looked at me apologetically.

I said, "Go with her. I really understand why she's so upset."

Several weeks went by. I didn't anticipate hearing from Heidi and Steven again. I doubted that Steven had the power to require Heidi to take her addiction seriously. Much to my surprise, one spring morning the phone rang and Heidi's sweet voice said, "May I have an appointment to see you?" I nearly fell off my chair. I thought perhaps Steven might come to discuss with me how he could cope with her addiction but, after Heidi's abrupt departure, I felt I was the last person she would want to see again. I gave her a time and Heidi came in faithfully every week for the next three years. She lived a long distance from my office. We arranged two-hour appointments once a week, as the commute took an hour and a half each way. Heidi was punctual. She never missed an appointment except when she was out of town or one of the children was very sick. (A little girl was born to them a year later, when Samuel was three and a half years old.)

During the time that Heidi was pregnant with Jennifer, she didn't touch cocaine. Not only did she not use drugs, she didn't ingest caffeine or sugar. A model pregnant woman, she planned to be just as careful for nine additional months while she nursed Jennifer. We were blessed, because Jennifer's conception gave us a chance to do some real talking about life and how to live it.

Heidi was very clear that she didn't want the children running away as young teenagers, using drugs, and being promiscuous sexually to get drugs. She knew something was terribly wrong in her upbringing. Though she loved her father and mother very much, she recognized that they were not the models she wanted to follow. The difficulty was she didn't have any idea of how normal people lived. She really thought that it was boring and wasteful to live a regular life.

Heidi had grown up in the world of fantasy where all the excitement occurred inside her head or in dialogue with her stuffed animals. That pattern easily translated into the excitement of the stage. As we worked, it became clear that the stage was her grownup version of fantasyland. She resented Steven, Samuel, and the new baby for requiring her attention so that she couldn't pursue her dream of being a great star. She felt time slipping away, taking beauty and youth, the prime prerequisites for making it as an actress.

Heidi was a beautiful young woman, dressed in the latest clothes worn by sophisticated New Yorkers. As she took care of Samuel and Jennifer, she imagined how it was going to be when the crowds roared their approval of her performance on Broadway. She could picture the newspaper write-ups, magazine covers, and admiring throngs.

I suggested, "Life is long and there is plenty of time to fulfill your dream of being a great actress. You need to settle down and give those two children a good start as they each have eighty years of life before them. If you fail them in their infancy, they will be permanently damaged. These precious months of being bonded with a kind, loving, empathic mother are crucial." Despite all our effort and technique, therapists will not ever be able to mirror a person into a stable personality as completely as a good-enough mother. A number of British psychologists and psychoanalysts have written about the importance of bonding in the first couple of years of a child's life. I referred her to Winnicott and Renee Spitz and Mahler and Bowlby to help Heidi understand infancy.

Every week she bucked like a young colt. She would come in yelling that nothing could be duller than boring old housewife-mother jobs. Made for greatness, she was stuck with middle America, cleaning spilled milk and tying shoelaces.

She referred over and over again, as the months went by, to my audacity in suggesting she give me Samuel. Each time I smiled sweetly and said, "I meant it. I would have tried to take your child if you hadn't begun to wrestle with your problem." I don't know if I could have taken Samuel. In fact, I doubted it; but my saying it scared her into dealing with reality. She began to search for a transformed life.

Heidi really didn't know anything about managing herself in this world. I had to teach her how to think, how to feel, how to believe. She had spent too much time as a youngster working and reworking the rapprochement with her mother, running away and coming back to emotional scenes, yelling and crying and running away again. She knew how to get away from internal pain as a youngster with fantasy and as an adolescent with drugs and sex, but she had never learned to live a stable, peaceful life. We talked and talked about how the peace that passes understanding can be achieved. Heidi was Jewish. Samuel attended preschool at the synagogue where he was carefully instructed in the faith.

Some of my evangelical brethren might think that I should have witnessed to her about Jesus, but that's not ethical. My job is to increase her faith, not convert her to mine. I talked to her a great deal, using people in the Old Testament because she had been well-trained as a child in Judaism. Heidi was not a practicing, synagogue-going Jew, but I had the feeling that Samuel's enthusiasm would draw her back into the faith. We knew a lot of the same people, all the folks in the Old Testament. Their deeds, their words, events that happened and their reactions were common knowledge.

Becoming Whole

Of course, Heidi didn't know she was being transformed. I had frightened her, so she kept coming back to see if she could figure out how to live a less-chaotic life for the sake of the children. We talked about all the people in the Bible who had totally changed their way of being in the world. Noah had to build his ark; Abraham had to leave the land of Ur. Jacob had to flee the wrath of his twin brother after he cheated him out of his birthright. His uncle cheated him out of the beautiful Rachel, until he'd worked an extra seven years. Jacob returned, wrestled with the angel who named him Israel, and reunited with his brother Esau twenty-one years later. Moses was raised in the Pharaoh's court the way Heidi had been raised in a very wealthy household. Then for forty years, he led the humdrum life of a shepherd before God called him through a burning bush to rescue his people. None of these men expected to be doing what they were doing. God's plan for people is to have us each do something that is absolutely different from anything we have done before to become whole, or holy.

After Jennifer was born, Heidi stayed completely drug-free until Jennifer was four months old. Then Heidi began to get restless.

"I don't want to nurse anymore; Jennifer really prefers the bottle. It is too much trouble having to hold her for hours at my breast. She is endlessly hungry."

"You are getting out of nursing to start using drugs again."

"No, that's not true. Jennifer needs more food than I can provide."

Heidi was a very slender girl. Through exercise and diet, she went back to her pre-pregnancy weight very quickly. I suspected that Jennifer wasn't getting enough food, because Heidi was reducing to feel comfortable as an actress.

My worst fears were realized. Within two weeks of weaning Jennifer, Heidi began doing lines of cocaine.

"I want the high. I need the excitement. Cocaine really picks me up. Steven and I enjoy using coke every night together. It really enhances sex. I am not using it all day. I'm keeping the house clean and watching the children so there's nothing to worry about!"

I worried. I really worried. I knew that she was an addictive personality. A little cocaine would lead to a lot of cocaine because it reduced her internal anxiety. Within several weeks she took both children and flew to Chicago. She also took the nurse to watch them while she used cocaine. I wasn't quite clear what she used for money, nor was her husband. She claims they gave it to her free. Heidi went on a wild weekend. For three days, twenty-four hours a day with the exception of a few moments of sleep, she free-based. At the end of the third day, her body suddenly went into a collapse. She couldn't breathe or move. Her heart was pounding. She knew she was dying and she was terrified.

The man who had been supplying the drug said to the other people around, "Get her out of here! I don't want her to die in my space!"

Weakly she whispered, "Please call an ambulance."

He replied, "Certainly not! I don't want the authorities to know we're using drugs in this apartment."

They bundled her up, took her down the stairs, and sat her out on the pavement. She still couldn't move, but luckily a cruising taxi driver stopped to ask if she was all right. He scooped her up and took her back to her relatives. They were appalled to find her in such terrible condition, though she was beginning to be able to move and breathe a little more easily.

That experience really frightened Heidi. She didn't know what it was in the cocaine that had produced such a violent reaction, but she never wanted to experience the paralysis again. She realized that she had nearly been one more statistic, dead of an overdose. Every time she looked at her children, she was horrified that her folly had almost deprived them of their mother. When she came back to me, she was determined to admit she was an addict and start living Narcotics Anonymous's twelve-step program.

Six months later, I'm glad to say that she is still clean. She and Steven bought a new home which has taken up her excess time and energy, painting and decorating. They found a street full of children so Samuel and Jennifer will have many friends. Teaching Heidi how to live like a normal person will be carried on by the parents of Samuel's and Jennifer's friends.

It's hard to imagine people growing up really not knowing how to live calm, productive lives. Heidi needed therapy to learn how to live. The panic at possibly losing Samuel galvanized her into searching for a new way of being in the world.

Heidi

Conclusion: Addictive personalities are very difficult to help. The drug, alcohol, food, sex, horses, gambling, buying, etc. keeps the individual from feeling panic and pain. They are the defenses against unconscious conflicts. One young man told me he had never been clean a day in his adult life. Sobriety meant all the identity confusion, self-consciousness, and mood swings of adolescence. It was painful, too painful!

Heidi grew up with parents who used liquor and pills to feel better. The Adult Children of Alcoholics national organization has come out with a number of books detailing the confusion children experience when parents use substances. Three rules are learned by these children: don't talk, don't trust, don't feel.

Heidi was a tough little kid; she was a survivor. Her response to the circus of her home, which couldn't give her needed emotional supplies, was to run away. By abusing herself with sex and drugs, Heidi acted out her rage at the lack of stable, loving, empathic care.

Nonetheless, she took good care of herself even when living on the streets. Heidi survived physically, wasn't raped, and was able, despite chaotic attendance, to finish high school. This was an amazing feat considering her tender years. She took what she wanted, making few friends in her struggle to survive. It never occurred to Heidi that she would ever want a normal life. Fame and fortune beckoned from every movie; stardom was hers for the asking. To be an actress became her goal.

Then Steven came along—and Samuel. Suddenly an independent roamer was tied down to bottles and diapers. She felt trapped, unable to quiet her internal anxiety through new adventures. Her dreams crashed into reality. Feeling deep love for Samuel and Steven, she found this discontent baffling. Heidi had chosen marriage and a family. She was very grateful for her home and healthy kids. To calm the increasing anxiety, Heidi turned to self-medication. She moved through her days—not talking, not trusting, not feeling. Her hopes to be an actress receded as her face and body aged. At twenty-four, she felt over the hill. More drugs to dull the pain seemed the only answer; she lived for her daily fixes.

A responsible parent, Heidi was able to stop cold while pregnant and nursing. The little person in her uterus gave her company and hope. Hormones naturally released kept her serene and cheerful. Not until she physically separated herself through weaning did the old internal restlessness resume. Heidi never learned to manage anxiety through crafts, hobbies, exercise, friends, synagogue work, political action, reading, taking classes, or the myriad of endeavors enjoyed by normal people. When others were learning those skills in childhood, Heidi was reenacting her separation-enmeshment crisis with her mother. Raging, she ran; longing, she returned. Hurt, she ran; wanting connection, she went home.

Never having received enough of her mom when she was very small, Heidi couldn't individuate into her own person. Life was severe anxiety and management of that anxiety—no games, or books, or deep friendships. When I met Heidi, her mom was still the most important person in her life. They talked every day by phone and visited frequently. Pleasing her mother was the most important factor in Heidi's decision-making. She feared her mom's criticism. Heidi quoted her mom to me frequently; she is a very opinionated woman. She is also very attractive and humorous and intelligent, which makes it even harder for Heidi to separate herself.

In long-term dynamic psychotherapy, the therapist enters into the unconscious of the patient. He or she becomes a supportive introject with whom the patient can dialogue. Heidi would say to me, "I talked this over with you in my head before I made a decision; I stopped and thought how you would suggest I handle Samuel's temper tantrum before I acted." I was always on Heidi's team, encouraging her from the sidelines to make creative choices. Her unique individuality came to maturity under my steady, encouraging guidance. She continued to enjoy the wonderful aspects of her mom and dad, but learned where they stopped and she began. Heidi could sort out her own answers to questions about what she wanted to do with her time and money.

Setting Limits

Individuation is crucial if we want to grow up to full maturity. Stunted development always causes dis-ease internally as the unfinished growth struggles toward completion. Junior fights to complete developmental tasks unfinished due to environmental pressures. As an infant Heidi had been intermittently mirrored by her mother, because pills altered her moods. The baby couldn't learn about her impact on the environment through her mother's facial expressions and verbalizations because her mother was inconsistent. Children need limits, clear guidelines indicating appropriate and inappropriate behavior. A substance user cannot set limits for himself; he is woefully inadequate at enforcing rules for youngsters.

A therapist can be consistent and available. As I listened to Heidi talk about her week's activities, she gained insights about how well she was making choices from hearing herself. Sometimes I would ask a question so she could see herself more clearly. As my mind's eye envisioned her daily activities while she reported them, discrepancies between her conscious desire to behave appropriately and her unconscious wishes would emerge. Since behavior is controlled by the unconscious, she was often bewildered by her own actions. We would carefully explore her dynamics to gain knowledge about why Heidi, like Saint Paul, did not understand what she did, for what she wanted to do, she did not do, but what she hated, she did (Romans 7:15). Looking through the perspective of the priorities we had clearly established for her life, detrimental decisions were highlighted. For example, if she really wanted the best for her children, she must stay away from drugs. She cannot use them recreationally as the frightening experience in Chicago demonstrated. Each time Heidi felt inadequate or guilty, we could discover the roots of those feelings and plan activities to cope with them.

Leaving a person enmeshed with his or her mother produces addictive behavior of some type. It is natural to become one's own person, working out one's own destiny; it creates an unconscious conflict to be attached to mother as an adult. Accurate mirroring by a therapist can resolve this rapprochement crisis and "proclaim freedom for the captives" (Isaiah 61:1; Luke 4:18).

Having a religious orientation was very helpful in Heidi's case. As a youngster, she had studied the stories of Israel, incorporating ways of thinking and valuing into her psyche. When reminded of them, she could understand what it means to be a Jew. Yahweh chose a particular people to be closely joined with Him. They would be examples for the world. Their dedication to doing God's will was the central fact of the patriarchs' lives. Prophets were sent out and ridiculed for speaking the Almighty's words. Martyrs met horrible deaths, confident in their righteousness: i.e., their right relationship with God.

The toys of this world faded into the background for Heidi once she began to re-study Scripture. Even family commitments became less important than knowing Yahweh. As Heidi went about her daily activities, her thoughts turned more and more to the God she saw in Israel's history. His power sustained her as she learned to be an adult in the real world without using drugs to escape. Ultimately mirrored by God, Heidi saw herself as a beloved daughter of the King of Kings.

"But we all, with open face beholding as in a glass the glory of the Lord, are changed into the same image from glory to glory, even as by the Spirit of the Lord" (2 Corinthians 3:18 KJV).

11
You've Got to Help Me

ROBIN

Synopsis: Desperate to find help after suicide attempts, hospitalizations, and bulimia programs, Robin came to the group. Working with dreams, she began to recover. Then she became pregnant. She tried to take her life again. An abortion was psychologically out of the question, so she went to live in a home for addicts. There she was cared for until Hannah was a year old. When she returned to her family in Virginia, Hannah was developmentally very advanced. Despite a brief setback with alcohol, now controlled through attendance at Alcoholics Anonymous meetings, Robin has overcome her crazily self-abusive behavior.

You've Got to Help Me

I met Robin for the first time at a bulimia meeting. She was a good-looking nineteen-year-old with sparkling blue eyes and long brown hair. She had lots of energy. Growing up comfortably in Virginia, she'd had a seemingly normal childhood. Robin's dad was a traveling salesman on the road about 50 percent of the time. Her mom had cleaning and babysitting help to make it a little easier to raise Robin.

When Robin came to the group, she told a terrifying story of hospitalizations, suicide attempts, drug abuse, and an unmanageable bulimic habit. She could eat six half-gallons of ice cream at a sitting, washed down with massive amounts of ginger ale to help her vomit. She consumed three pies, a cake, four hamburgers, and a dozen donuts all in one sitting, interspersed with purging. Her habit was costing $125 a day. It took all her time, except when she was teaching swimming. Her vomiting started in high school, so her education suffered. With low grades and poor academic skills, she couldn't go to college.

Robin heard about our group from a friend. The first night she begged, "You've got to help me. I have been to so many groups and so many programs I can't even count them anymore. None of them have worked! Please!"

She readily agreed to come faithfully every week to work dreams. She always participated enthusiastically in the conversation and began to have fewer episodes.

Two months later she came to group one night looking terrible. She confessed to having again tried to take her life because she was pregnant. She thought it was better to kill herself with pills than try to tell her parents about her sexual indiscretion. They would be furious at a pregnancy without marriage.

Have Your Baby

For a girl who already feels empty inside, a pregnancy is very precious. They know someone is there inside, a longed-for companion. Having an abortion feels like something that is hers to protect is being ripped away. For Robin, the panic states were so great that, despite her upper-class appearance, internally she was living a nightmare.

I told her I didn't believe it was healthy for her to have an abortion. She had already had one and was emotionally devastated for months afterwards. She could decide during the pregnancy whether she wanted to keep the infant or give it up for adoption, but her psychological condition was such that abortion was out of the question. She said that her mother and father would throw her out if they found out she was pregnant without being married; she could not support herself. I told her that I knew of a home in which she could stay, a half-way house for recovering addicts.

Robin moved in the next day. She was a delightful addition to the household, always cheerful, enthusiastic, helpful, and cooperative. The time flew by. One night after a bulimia meeting she said, "I think I'll go to the hospital now." A friend drove her over, coached her through her labor, and took her home before noon the next day.

Hannah was a sturdy little girl though it took Robin five days to teach her how to nurse. I had forgotten the complicated process involved if a youngster doesn't get the hang of it right away. The doctor suggested beer to get her milk flowing. Robin called me the first day to ask, "How do I put a diaper on this baby?" I was a little startled, because before the birth of my first child, I had carefully studied every book and practiced on a friend's newborn. I had forgotten the obsessive personality's inability to anticipate. Taking responsibility is very difficult for people with bulimia.

As the weeks progressed, Hannah taught Robin how to be a good mother. I suggested she always keep the baby with her. She slept with her at night and carried her around all day. She was never put in another room for a nap or confined to a playpen. They breathed, ate, slept, and walked four hours a day together. Hannah thrived. The other people living in the house thoroughly enjoyed playing with Hannah. When Robin had to take a shower, or needed a few minutes by herself, the baby easily passed from hand to hand, smiling at her many friends.

After Hannah was born, Robin began to talk to her mother and father. Previously, each time her parents called, they expressed their vehement disapproval. Being pregnant without a husband was unthinkable! Hannah's father was a young man Robin had known for years. They had been best friends in high school. They didn't feel ready for marriage, though they cared very much about each other. Slowly her parents began to accept the situation and look forward to meeting Hannah.

After three months Robin said she thought she really should work to support herself. I applauded her sense of responsibility for herself and Hannah and her willingness to work to support them, but I reminded her that infants are devastated when their mothers are away from them. I urged her to stay at the half-way house and play with her new baby until the little one was two years of age.

Children who were not well-bonded as infants tend to have real difficulty bonding with their own babies. Bonding means a sense between the mother and the child that they are one person. Ideally this feeling continues during the first twenty-four months. The mother knows what the baby is thinking. The capacity to bond an infant depends on chemicals released at birth in all women. They can understand their babies during the long period when the little ones cannot let us know what's happening. This ability is enhanced through close physical proximity to the baby day and night for the first two years. Biologically, new mothers have a drive to watch their babies all the time. As they watch, they learn the small clues that tell the infant's needs and desires. When a mother and child bond well, the youngster feels very safe in the world. He grows up with a sense that the universe is trustworthy and his needs are important because Mother reacts appropriately.

The early bonded relationship is the prototype for the relationship we yearn for as adults. Unfortunately, never again in this life do we have anyone resonating as closely as a bonded mother, sublimating herself for us. Sometimes for a short period of time we may attempt to recapture that original feeling with our mothers through a relationship with a lover. That intense need to be with another person who fully understands and accepts us just as we are, and is fascinated by our "little toes" as well as every word that comes out of our lips, is a desire well publicized by television and romantic novels.

We enter into marriage hoping for the remembered intimate union. There are brief moments, of course, but that kind of fascination with someone is usually gone within a year. Scott Peck says we wake up one morning and wonder who the stranger is next to us in bed.

The Lost Art of Mothering

Since the Second World War, most women in America have been distracted from their babies. They want to look slim and beautiful. They want to go back to work. They want time for entertainment with their husbands. They want to keep a perfect house. They want to keep up with their neighbors, as they did before the baby was born. Many influences tear young mothers away from their young.

Infants should be raised by calm, quiet mothers who have nothing else to do except play with their babies. In igloos, in African huts, in Mexican villages, all over the Third World, infants are being raised properly. Only in Western civilization have we taken the baby off the mother's back and put it in a crib. Only in so-called enlightened nations have infants been required to wait between feedings, alone, in a room apart from the rest of the family.

This kind of cruelty to infants has led to a massive rise in anxiety and characterological disorders which feeds a vast army of psychologists, psychiatrists, social workers, and marriage and family counselors. We truly live in an age of anxiety because the skills of mothering have been lost. Many women think they're somehow shirking their responsibilities if they're not back in the work force by the time the infant is three months of age. The cost in psychological damage to mother and child is enormous.

Unfortunately, Robin's mother had not been able to nurse her. Nursing on demand allows the mother and child to spend lots of time together as the milk is drawn much more slowly out of the breast than out of a bottle. Infants like to suck and sleep and suck again, safe in their mother's arms.

Robin's mother had been taught that children would be spoiled if they were picked up when they cried. Crying was normal and children should be made to wait at least three and a half hours between feedings, and they should learn to sleep through the night at an early age. She tried to make Robin conform to the norms in the baby books. Robin's screaming protests made her mother even more anxious, resulting in a strained relationship.

Luckily this didn't happen to Hannah because she was always with Robin, waking and sleeping. They became one. When Hannah slept, Robin slept. When Hannah woke, Robin fed her and took her out for long walks.

Unfortunately, Robin continued to drink beer. She was nursing so she knew better than to binge and purge but beer seemed all right. The doctor told her that beer would increase her milk. It worried the group because bulimics often turn into alcoholics, and vice-versa. One day when Hannah was about six months old, Robin was coming down the stairs to a bulimia meeting. She tripped and nearly dropped the baby. Those of us standing at the foot of the stairs were horrified at how close the infant had come to being killed. We confronted Robin about her drinking and suggested she join Alcoholics Anonymous. She did and soon was working the organization's twelve steps of recovery successfully.

Hannah Won't Need a Therapist

We supported Robin while her baby was little. When Robin returned to her family home, they continued to support her until Hannah was two. Then she was old enough to go to a daycare center while Robin went back to work as a swimming instructor. Hannah loved playing with the other children. Robin's parents enjoyed having their charming, intelligent granddaughter around. Hannah was very advanced for her age. Because Robin had been available, she attended to training her body and brain without anxiety, as God planned for all children.

Hannah will not need a therapist when she grows up. In this age of anxiety, she will be an adult who calmly and cheerfully knows her own mind, trusting that the universe is benevolent. She won't have any difficulty relating to a God who knows and loves her. In the midst of difficulties and trials, Hannah will have a sure sense that all things work together for good, because she was held and carried in the formative first two years of her life. Because her mother was always there for her, she won't have any difficulty realizing God is always there for her, even when things go badly. As her mother picked her up when she got hurt, so she will know that God lifts us when life injures. The hunger born in each of us at birth to be at one with another human being was met by Robin's continual presence. She knows that the nurturing, feeding person will never abandon her; she is safe.

Our Jealous God's Yearnings

As we mature, we yearn for the Garden of Eden, that happy place where we are at one with someone else. A great deal of deodorant and mouthwash and cruises and cars are sold on the premise that if you have the right look and smell, a mysterious other will appear with whom one can be totally connected. But it's a myth, a great falsehood! Nobody ever again knows us completely, accepts us utterly, and is always there for us, except God. No adult person can duplicate the intimacy of a good mother.

God arranged it this way as He is jealous, yearning to have each of us in an ongoing, intense, passionate relationship with Him. He is not interested in our being so enmeshed with another human being that our needs are met. He wants us for Himself; He wants our minds continually turned toward Him. When we hear His call and make Him the central relationship of our lives, resentment and bitterness that others won't give us what we want diminish. Priorities fall into place. We can live a life of joy and peace that passes understanding.

When the woman caught in adultery was brought before Him, Jesus said that he who is without sin should throw the first stone. That was an unexpected word. The Pharisees and Sadducees had really hoped to trap Him in a legalistic dispute. Instead, He spoke about forgiveness and the common sinfulness of all people.

Some church folk condemned me for treating an unmarried, pregnant, young woman as if she were one of my daughters. It seemed to them that I was condoning sin and giving a bad example to other young people. I can only say that for me the time of watching Robin grow was one of great joy. Robin and Hannah enriched my life and the lives of those with whom they stayed. The enthusiasm I feel when God directs me to do something like support Robin is a sign of His will in my life. I won't cast a stone.

Last month Robin called. Hannah is six years old. She's doing very well in first grade at a superior school, has many friends, and is the star of her swimming team. Robin works at a bank, and enjoys overseeing one of the departments. She has been living with her family, appreciating them more and more each day. Robin phoned to tell me she was getting married in two days to a wonderful man who loved Hannah. She wanted to thank me for saving her life.

Robin

Conclusion: A pregnancy calmed Robin's internal hell. United with the little one before and after birth, quieted physically by nature's hormones, Robin's panics subsided. During her two years in the group, Robin learned better defenses to handle anxiety. Humor, altruism (helping others), anticipation (planning for the future), sublimation (attending to activities that are positive rather than dwelling on the negative), and suppression (forgetting about problems we cannot solve) became available ways to stop the vomiting. A brief slide into another compulsive behavior— drinking—stopped when she began working the program of Alcoholics Anonymous.

Hannah thrived through closeness with her mom. She was the center of Robin's attention for two years. Hannah was so charming and calm, her grandparents also found her a delight when they moved home. God intends that we be reconciled, living at peace with parents and children. Robin would always have resented her parents if she'd had to give up Hannah. Fulfilling her biological destiny gave her a sense of completion and self-approval which quieted Junior.

As a Christian, I disapprove of sexual intercourse outside of marriage. But also as a Christian, I can love the sinner, helping her cope with the consequences of her sin. Robin and Hannah blessed the half-way house, drawing together the distressed young people. Everyone enjoyed being Hannah's family; her smile taught them all to rise above their troubles. Looking into her innocent brown eyes, addicts living there had to reevaluate their priorities. I am sure God sent them the young mother and her infant, reminding them of the young one in Bethlehem. He knew about irregular situations and God's mercy.

Robin became a strong Christian, praying and reading the Bible every day. At two, Hannah could sing "Jesus loves me, this I know." Her sweetness gave God the glory.

"But if we walk in the light, as he is in the light, we have fellowship one with another, and the blood of Jesus Christ his son cleanseth us from all sin" (1 John 1:7 KJV).

12
Let Him Die Joyfully

PHILIP

Synopsis: The baby was dying of a brain tumor. His parents came to learn how best to manage the enormous physical and emotional stress of a terminal illness. With great courage and grace, the Loewens turned their son's death into a shining example of creative living. A group of families meeting weekly to share about children and death helped them maintain equanimity. A deeper appreciation for each day, with all its joys and frustrations, was born in all of us as Philip died.

Let Him Die Joyfully

I met Philip when he was seven months old. He was sitting on his mother's lap while his two-year-old sister played nearby. His mom and dad came to see me because Philip had an inoperable brain tumor. The doctors were not very hopeful about saving his life. As a last resort, they were trying an experimental drug. Surgery hadn't removed all the malignancy. Philip looked terrific —a round, handsome, cheerful baby, sitting up and looking around at the world with eager eyes. He was still nursing and clearly had a marvelous relationship with his mom and dad.

His parents knew I had done a good deal of work with families of children who were dying. They were very concerned about how they should manage the fact that Philip might be dying. No one in their respective families had been seriously ill. The diagnosis of a terminal illness is a traumatic shock; learning how to cope emotionally comes slowly afterwards.

As we talked I found these parents managed life very successfully. Coming from good homes, they were psychologically stable and had a good relationship. Bob had gone through law school. After Jacinta graduated from college, they fell in love and married. They eagerly looked forward to their first baby when Jacinta became pregnant. Their child was born without a brain. In medical language, that's called anencephalic. There was no warning. Jacinta went into the hospital expecting a normal child and found out after she delivered that the infant would die. Little Jenifer lived three days; the sorrowing parents went home with empty arms.

They were young and soon a healthy little girl was born to them. They named her Kimberly. She was a delight, bright and strong. Two years later, Philip came along. He was as sturdy and responsive as Kimberly had been. Needless to say, they were thrilled. Philip grew and prospered, loving to nurse and play. Then, at a routine visit to the pediatrician, they were told that Philip's head was growing too rapidly. After many tests came the dreaded diagnosis, a malignant brain tumor. Philip was six months old.

The parents researched the best medical centers in the country and finally took him to The Brain Tumor Research Center in San Francisco. Everything was done that could be done. Surgery was performed and further tests given leading ultimately to the conclusion that the tumor could not be stopped.

As they sat before me that Sunday afternoon, my job was to give hope and comfort in the midst of this devastating situation. We spent three hours together, and I questioned them intensively about all the circumstances that had occurred prior to our meeting. I wanted to know about their marriage, Kimberly's birth, Bob's work, how they got along, all the joys they were having parenting Kimberly, Jenifer's birth and death, and how they handled the grieving.

Then I wanted to know all about Philip, from the time he was conceived to the time he was born, how they felt, what they saw, what they enjoyed, what the hospital room was like, what baby clothes they brought him home in, everything. In the meantime, while I was asking all these questions, Philip cooed and gurgled and nursed and played with toys. Kimberly bounced around the room.

I Guess My Son Will Die

Everyone talks at approximately five hundred words a minute; we think at the rate of two thousand words a minute. For me, much of that fifteen-hundred-word differential is always spent in prayer. I want to speak God's word to people sitting in my office. The only way I'll discern it correctly is if I listen, keeping myself an open channel. As the Loewens sat before me, I was actively pleading with God for the right words.

The Loewens were not Christians. They had rejected God and all the trappings of the church years before, but I knew that God had not rejected them. He was anxious at this bitter time in their lives to give them the balm of Gilead through me.

I asked them, "What do you think is going to happen?"

Bob replied, "We hope Philip is going to live."

"I hope so, too. He is a beautiful child. If he doesn't live, then what will happen?"

They looked at me as if I were stupid. "I guess he'll die."

After a pause, Bob repeated, "I guess my son will die."

"Yes, I guess he will," I echoed. "What are you going to do for fun between now and then so that if he does die, you will have had a joyful time?"

They both looked at me in absolute astonishment. Jacinta asked, "How can we have fun when our baby might be dying?"

Emphatically, I replied, "Very carefully! By choosing to give Philip, Kimberly, and yourselves good experiences, you will always remember this period of your lives with satisfaction. If Philip dies, you will know that you gave him a happy time. If he lives, you will not regret the adventures you shared."

Jacinta remarked, "We've both been so sad and worried, we've even forgotten how to laugh."

"That's what I thought. Begin laughing today! Does anybody know a joke?"

We told a couple of jokes, a couple of stupid knock-knock jokes, and we laughed. Hearing laughter again, Kimberly lit up like a Christmas tree.

"Why don't you take Philip to Hawaii with your video camera? Kimberly would enjoy visiting her grandmother."

Bob replied, "Good idea! I'll take off from work. We'll go right away because Philip may get sick again. Now's a good time for us to play!"

Once that was settled, I asked, "Are you afraid about anything?"

Softly, Jacinta said, "Yes, we're afraid about how he's going to die."

"What about his dying scares you?"

Jacinta had tears in her eyes. "The doctors say he'll stop eating. I don't think I can bear to see my child starve to death. The doctors recommend that when the tumor turns off the appetite center in his brain, we put a tube down his nose and feed him."

"Why are you afraid of Philip starving to death? It's not a painful way to die."

They were amazed. It had never occurred to them that dying by starvation was not acutely painful.

"If Philip is going to die anyway, prolonging his life for another few weeks might not be kind. Feeding him through a tube down his nose will reduce the quality of his life. Kids hate NG tubes irritating their throats."

Bob said, "I know we do not want any extraordinary measures. Having Philip in the hospital tied up to machines, kept alive by artificial means, would be terrible. Are you suggesting that Philip might be able to die at home?"

We talked at some length about children dying in countries around the world without access to medical facilities. They are poor, in that they do not have access to medical facilities, but rich, in that they are not separated from their parents as they lie dying.

Hospice work had taught me how much more comfortable home is for the terminally ill whenever possible.

Celebrating a Little Life

Bob and Jacinta were greatly relieved. If Philip had to die, they were pleased they'd be able to give him a life which maintained its quality to the very end. They walked out of my office with knowledge and courage for the ordeal ahead. Within two weeks of our discussion, they went to Hawaii with Philip. Their video film taken on that vacation was shown on a recent HBO special that included Philip's story.

Every week they came to our Candlelighters' meeting where parents of children who are dying or have died gathered together to share their bewilderment, sorrow, and rage. They talked about ways to handle themselves and situations. We supported the Loewens as Philip gradually weakened. Jacinta kept him close to her all day. Bob cared for him when he wasn't working. Philip slept in bed with them every night. He was a cheerful child. Two days before he died, I carried Philip around for awhile as different people in the group were talking, and thanked him quietly for being such a very special person in all our lives. Though he was really ten months old, he looked like a little starving baby as he hadn't been able to eat for the last three weeks. His enchanting smile was still in place and a great feeling of calm came from his small body. I knew he was going to a place where he'd be given a perfect body to fit his bright and shining soul.

A week later a memorial service for Philip was held in a park right by his house. More than a hundred people gathered to affirm the impact Philip's short life had had on them. I said a few words about my belief that the life set before us is greater and more wonderful than any experience on this earth. Philip was in a far happier place where he could run and dance and sing. We will see Philip again. He has gone before us to find all the best places to play.

His father told how meaningful it had been to live the adventure of Philip's dying. His short life had brought understanding about how crucial it was to practice joyful living every day. Philip taught us not to be afraid.

Afterwards songs were sung and many people spoke. Joined together in a circle, we released balloons with notes to Philip tied on the strings. It was a lovely sight when all those colors rose into a very blue sky and then drifted slowly away.

Bob and Jacinta handled a terrible tragedy with courage and creativity. Instead of using the few remaining months of Philip's life to keep their family and friends in a state of misery, the Loewens managed wisely. Using resources drawn from character, which as we know comes from suffering (Romans 5:3-4), they handled the loss of a second child with dignity and grace.

Philip

Conclusion: The Loewens are not Christians. They were turned off by bad church experiences as youngsters. Many followers of the living Christ would not have been able to deal creatively, without self-pity, with Philip's dying. They sought guidance in handling Philip physically and psychologically. Once they gained perspective, Bob and Jacinta dedicated themselves to making the remaining time a positive experience.

Jesus also faced certain death. Andrew G. Hodges, a Christian psychiatrist (*Jesus: An Interview Across Time: A Psychiatrist Looks at His Humanity*) believes Jesus knew by age twelve He would die on a cross. The ecclesiastical establishment's irritation was bound to have dire consequences. Like the Loewens, Jesus lived in the shadow of death.

Jesus came among us to teach victorious, God-centered living. What did He do with His time, we may ask, while He waited to die? He went to a wedding, ate with various people, talked to friends and large groups, spent time alone in the mountains, laughed, cried, played with children, did miracles, prayed—He lived every day to the fullest. He lived joyfully, celebrating the Jewish high feasts with food and wine even on the night He was arrested. He stood silent before His accusers, not justifying Himself or asking for sympathy.

Facing death, many Christians, as well as non-Christians, become filled with self-pity; resentment that this terrible thing is happening makes them bitter. Continually filled with obsessive thoughts, trying magically to remove the bitter cup, they pour out their rage and anguish to all who will listen. Rather than evolve a plan to redeem the time, they weep and whine.

Looking Straight in the Face of Death

The Loewens were pragmatists. They believed in facts and probabilities. They knew they could make choices. Many Christians believe that God will remove the difficulty if they say the right prayer or pray long and hard enough. Some fast to persuade God to give them what they want. The church is seen as a pipeline to God, assuring His attention to their desires. They know what God should do. The Almighty is careless or inattentive because He allows children to die. If they can find a healer to intercede, God will perform a miracle. If the whole congregation prays, terminal illness will be reversed.

This is very poor theology. Jesus told us that miracles come from prayer and fasting (Mark 9:29) and that we should pray continually (1 Thessalonians 5:17). But prayer is to conform our minds to the mind of Christ, aligning our will with His. God suffers excruciating pain over the death of each infant; He counts the hairs on our heads (Luke 12:7), but for His inscrutable reasons He sometimes allows evil to triumph on the earth. The church should pray and fast individually and corporately, but for God's will to be done, not ours. Unfortunately, many never learn to love God for Himself, instead of for what He can do for them. Mystics and saints are passionately involved with our Creator because of His awesome majesty and holiness. They bless Him because He has already blessed us by His death on the cross. Those who seek to possess the mind of Christ are prepared for hardships and grief in this world. They know it is a training school, a boot camp, for victorious kingdom living.

Many Candlelighters came to us using other kinds of "magic" besides prayer. One mother kept two ceramic blue angels on her bureau. She believed as long as both angels were there, her son, stricken with osteogenic cancer, would live. Affirmations of hope, such as "I know he will live," and refusal to allow thoughts of death to enter the mind, are magic-working. Pretending the child is recovering, singing a certain song repetitively, and planning for the distant future are encouraged by groups who insist positive thinking alters the course of all cancers.

The Loewens, on the other hand, looked straight into the face of death to plan for Philip's living. They were equally as concerned for Kimberly, relatives, friends, and themselves. They worked through the options, and chose to prioritize their mental health. In his dying, Philip was a contented baby. Not knowing about the future, he was comfortable being close to his mom. His last days weren't spent crying from the pain of tests and shots and a tube down his throat. He rested peacefully with his family in familiar surroundings, listening to everyday sounds. All was very well for him.

Bob and Jacinta contained their frustration and grief. They remained adults, parents, everlasting arms for Philip and Kimberly. All of us were blessed by their wisdom and compassion as they ministered to Candlelighters despite their severe stress. I saw true heroism and I am grateful.

"Suffer little children, and forbid them not, to come unto me: for of such is the kingdom of heaven" (Matthew 19:14 KJV).

"'Tis the hardest thing in the world to give up everythin'; even though 'tis usually the only way to get everythin'."

"Why do people have to lose things to find out what they mean?"

"When ye love someone deeply, anything is possible—even miracles."

—*Brigadoon*

POSTSCRIPT

I wrote this book to shed some light on Christian psychotherapy. Over the years many people have asked me to explain how to evaluate case material and encourage change. I hope these case histories have been illustrative.

Secular psychotherapies have various goals in mind about the optimal human condition. Freud said a well-analyzed patient would be sadder and wiser. Our youthful optimism is tempered by a clear-eyed appraisal of reality; for Freud joy and naïveté are correlated. Wisdom comes from managing ourselves through self-knowledge. Heinz Kohut, a modern Freudian, states that a person must become self-soothing and self-stimulating. Instead of expecting the environment to comfort or encourage us, we must learn to look to ourselves.

Followers of Wilhelm Reich postulate an ideal state in which, our body armor dissolved, we will be fully in touch with our physical and emotional needs. Humanists like Carl Rogers hypothesized that being aware of our actual selves, previously buried under our adaptive selves, would allow us to live congruently. Existentialists, like Fritz Perls, encourage people to stay in their here-and-now, freed from restricting "shoulds" and "oughts." Once liberated from an overly scrupulous superego through therapy, men and women would enjoy being themselves. Berne said happiness could come from understanding the games people play. Self-actualization was the end goal for Maslow and Erikson. Self-esteem, creative fulfillment, enriched relationships through better communications promised the good life.

Therapists who studied family systems, like Bower, Wittaker, Minuchin and Satir, were convinced that developing appropriate family systems could produce comfortable living. They built on the earlier work of Harry Stack Sullivan and Karen Horney, among others. Karl Marx was convinced economic equality would bring happiness. Behavior modifiers from Watson to Skinner taught us how to train clients to act differently, believing that inappropriate learning produced poor adjustment to life. Behavior which advanced society's commonly accepted standards was encouraged.

Since man first began to think abstractly, the question of what is good has been pondered by philosophers and theologians alike. It must be answered by therapists as well, because value systems impact their work. Despite efforts to be aware of countertransference (our own feelings in the sessions) and our ethical attempts not to influence our clients' value systems, the material we choose to emphasize in each session impacts their frames of reference.

For example, if a therapist believes women must stand up for their rights, her female patients will be affirmed for self-affirmation. If a clinician agrees that sitting at one's desk in third grade is good, then the child client will be rewarded for seat time, overtly or covertly. If a therapist feels men are bullheaded, she will communicate that belief to her patient.

A Christian believes each person is uniquely created and personally loved by God. Our natural selves continue to think and act in ways that separate us from our Heavenly Father. For example, we think we can run our own lives, love people we enjoy, and find happiness in toys, families, power, or money. Our "old man/

woman" really believes we should be happy and comfortable. When we're not, we rush to find a magic pill or book or relationship. God is seen as Santa Claus in the sky. Prayer is persuading Him to give us what we want.

God Lives in the Unexpected

Christians know that to find the "peace that passes understanding" and true joy, we have to lose ourselves. "What good is it for a man to gain the whole world, and yet lose or forfeit his very self?" (Luke 9:25). "It is easier for a camel to go through the eye of a needle than for a rich man to enter the kingdom of God" (Matthew 19:24). "For whoever wants to save his life will lose it, but whoever loses his life for me will save it" (Luke 9:24). "Go, sell everything you have . . . then come, follow me" (Mark 10:21). We are called to "hunger and thirst for righteousness" (Matthew 5:6). "Seek first his kingdom and his righteousness, and all these things will be given to you as well" (Matthew 6:33).

Losing ourselves is not common sense. We know God lives in the unexpected word, action, and circumstance. The Bible is full of stories of people to whom unusual, and sometimes even bizarre, circumstances occurred. Adam and Eve found themselves in the Garden of Eden enjoying God's company daily. They broke the one rule and found themselves outside, condemned to sweat and pain. In the beginning, each of us finds himself in a garden, rocked on our mother's breast. Protected by her vigilance, we are secure until the day we begin to oppose her will. At two years of age, we begin the process of individuation, symbolized by the word "no." The child's inevitable disobedience, breaking the parent's rules, drives him to fend for himself emotionally away from the safe, maternal breast. Survival then depends on the sweat of his brow in school as he painfully learns life's lessons.

Cain and Abel took sibling rivalry to its logical extension. One killed the other over an issue of who was favored—whom God (the parent for a child) loved best. Murder was the response to the universal fear—does Mommy, God, love me more than my brother?

How about Noah, poor man, going cheerfully about his business until God tells him that He's had enough of the foolishness of people? He's going to wipe them out. They are hard-hearted, unwilling to respond to Him in a graceful dance of mutual blessing. He wants to save the animals while destroying man. Imagine the ridicule that must have been heaped on Noah's head as he went about the unexpected act of building an enormous ark and collecting animals in the midst of a dry desert. It didn't make sense.

Or Abram, called out of the land of Ur in his old age. All his friends, his church connections, his business networks, his extended family, all cut off so that he could go wander in the desert. How unexpected! How peculiar! His neighbors must have said, "He's gone off his rocker." Even his wife wagged her head. She laughed when the angels told her she would bear a son. She was, after all, forty years past menopause. She had given her servant to Abram to bear an heir because she was barren. Then God said that Ishmael, who was heir to all that Abraham owned, was to be driven out into the desert. Righteousness was accounted to Abraham because he was obedient and did as he was told, almost killing Isaac. If Sarah had known what he was planning to do, she would have been sure that the old man had gone right off his rocker.

Jesus kept doing unexpected things, like washing people's feet, talking to women (even prostitutes), healing until He got tired, and then rowing away. He calmed storms with words and walked on water. He fed five thousand people from scraps of lunches he'd collected. He wouldn't take power although some disciples tried to talk Him into it. One Sunday He rode into Jerusalem on an ass to shouts of "Hosanna!" Then He chose to be crucified. Most people, on that dark Friday, were pretty sure He wasn't the Messiah, even though the temple veil was suddenly torn in half and darkness filled the sky at noon. The scientists explained about eclipses and earthquakes. Later the military people said His followers had stolen His body from the grave. It was very bewildering and unexpected.

How about those crazy guys at Pentecost talking to the Jews who were gathered from many different countries? They all heard about the risen Christ in their own language. Those foolish men turned into powerful champions of the faith, spreading it throughout the civilized world in a hundred years. Saint Paul was hardly your courageous type and yet something happened so that a rabbinical scholar turned into a mighty lion of God, enduring sufferings and persecutions. He established churches all over the known world.

Unexpected words, actions, and circumstances have changed the course of individual and collective history. I believe God plans the unexpected for our salvation. Our "old man/woman" clings to the understood and the familiar; but for growth to occur, we must be broken and changed. For holiness, our total trust needs to be in God, not in any of the circumstances of this life. Our response to change, whether painful or joyful, should be a shout of praise. God loves us enough to mold us at the Potter's wheel, to burn the dross away through unexpected happenings (Isaiah 64:8;1:25).

If we are not afraid of the unexpected in counseling, the therapeutic miracle occurs. Listening to God with one ear often results in hearing myself say things to clients I didn't know I knew. God gives specific interpretations and interventions if we'll wait for His words rather than follow common sense.

Jeanie hit the wall through postpartum depression. Intensive therapy allowed her to bond her infant and manage her feelings. David stopped asking his wife for sex, gave up his childish hope for a significant other, and turned to God for intimacy. Marcie learned to expect harmony, peace, and courtesy every day. She took control of the children despite her habitual practice of encouraging uproar, learned from her parents. Max worked hard in therapy to uncover rage and abandonment feelings created when his mother died, still influencing his reactions to women. When the depression occurred, he was helpless, allowing therapeutic exploration. Ann grew up enough to love her own company, giving up the expectation of nurturing created by infantile diabetes. Jonathan followed his enthusiasm into golf.

Thea had to radically change her relationship with her bulimic daughter if she wanted to see her grandchild. The shift effected the miracle of good parenting for Michelle's infant. Ray received hard knocks through a difficult child and a dissolving marriage. Working with disturbed youngsters gave him new ways of being with his family.

Francie was sliding deeper and deeper into mental invalidism. Guarded secrets, finally discovered in the unconscious, created the therapeutic miracle. Heidi had to be taught how normal people act and react. She knew her addictive ways precluded her being a good parent.

Robin controlled her behavior through the miracle of an infant daughter. Careful listening and a word of caution kept her from self-mutilation. Philip's death brought new life to his family because they were able to change their feelings about living and dying.

Each of the cases discussed in this book came out well. Unfortunately, sometimes people leave therapy prematurely, or are unable to face making the necessary changes. I look after them sadly. As I often say to my staff, "We are not here to fix people. We do not have the wisdom or power. We are here to mirror them accurately and speak God's healing words. Those who have ears to hear, will hear. We are here to love, as Jesus loved us. Those He calls will respond."

> I asked God for strength
> that I might achieve.
> I was made weak
> that I might learn humbly to obey.
>
> I asked for health
> that I might do greater things.
> I was given infirmity
> so that I might do better things.
>
> I asked for riches
> that I might be happy.
> I was given poverty
> that I might be wise.
>
> I asked for power
> that I might have the praise of men.
> I was given weakness
> that I might feel the need of God.

I asked for all things
that I might enjoy life.
I was given life
that I might enjoy all things.

I got nothing
that I asked for,
but everything I had hoped for.

For almost despite myself,
my unspoken prayers were answered.
I, among all, am most richly blessed.

(Prayer of a Confederate Soldier)

Appendix A

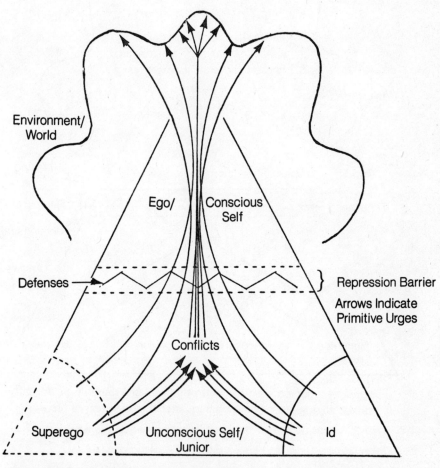

Diagram of a person who has characterological problems stemming from inadequate bonding in the first three years of life (pre-oedipal, personality disorders, borderline conditions).

Courtesy of Warren Jones, M.D., Ph.D.

153

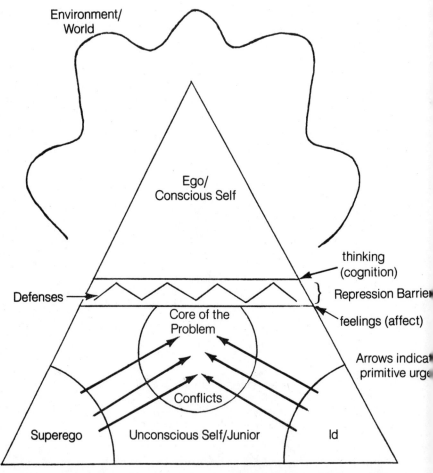

Diagram of a person who has neurotic problems stemming from difficulties occurring during development after the third year of life.

Courtesy of Warren Jones, M.D., Ph.D.

154

Appendix B

GLOSSARY

ABANDONMENT ANXIETY/ABANDONMENT FEAR: Mixed feelings of dread and apprehension that one will ultimately be deserted by those one loves and/or attempts to love, but without a specific current cause for this fear. Typically, such persons have experienced significant losses of and/or separations from parents and/or significant others during infancy or childhood.

ACTUALIZE: *see* SELF-ACTUALIZATION.

ADDICTIVE PERSONALITY: Specifically, a type of individual who has lost the power of self-control in relation to the use of drugs and/or alcohol and whose behavior has become largely determined by the use of these substances. More generally, a type of individual who exhibits significant compulsive and overpowering tendencies to engage in specific behaviors (i.e., eating, drug use, sex, gambling, etc.) in an unmanageable and self-abusive fashion.

ADULT: The term employed by Eric Berne to describe that consistent pattern of feeling, experience, and behavior of an individual (i.e., ego state) that is "oriented toward objective, autonomous data-processing and probability estimating" (Berne, 1966, p. 36).

AFFECT: "A broad class of mental processes, including feeling, emotion, moods, and temperament" (Chaplin, 1975, p. 14).

AGITATION: A tension state in which a person's anxiety is expressed through extreme restlessness, disorganization, irritability, and/or argumentativeness.

AGORAPHOBIA: "The dread of open spaces. The patient becomes panic-stricken, sometimes at the thought of, but more often at the impending visit to an open space. As a reaction against such an eventuality, he generally remains indoors and prefers to be at home, near the mother or someone possessing a kind, helpful, guiding influence" (Campbell, 1981, p. 19).

155

ALTRUISM (an ego defense): *see also* HAASS. One of the five "higher level defenses." Attending to the interests, needs, and problems of others rather than focusing solely on one's own problems, needs, and interests.

ANALYZING THE TRANSFERENCE: The process by which a patient's therapist will continually monitor and, when appropriate, make an interpretation of a patient's thoughts and feelings about the therapist to the patient in order to assist the patient in clarifying which of these are from his primitive/infantile nature (i.e., "residual from Junior") and which are part of his mature self.

ANOREXIA/ANOREXIA NERVOSA: An illness characterized by preoccupation with body weight, behaviors directed toward losing weight, and intense fear of gaining weight. "Anorexia nervosa occurs typically in females between the ages of 12 and 21; it has been reported also, however, in older women and men (in which case impotence seems to be a cardinal feature)" (Campbell, 1981, p. 39).

ANTICIPATION (an ego defense): *see also* HAASS. One of the five "higher level defenses." The ability of a person to foresee, experience, and deal with events or decisions beforehand through the use of imagination. "Anticipation of the future is characteristic of the ego and is necessary for judgment and planning of suitable later action" (Campbell, 1981, p. 41).

ANXIETY: "An affect that differs from other affects in its specific unpleasurable characteristics. Anxiety consists of a somatic, physiological side (disturbed breathing, increased heart activity, vasomotor changes, musculoskeletal disturbances such as trembling or paralysis, increased sweating, etc.) and of a psychological side. . . . Fear is a reaction to a real or threatened danger, while anxiety is more typically a reaction to an unreal or imagined danger" (Campbell, 1981, pp. 41–42).

ASSERTION TRAINING/ASSERTIVENESS TRAINING: "A procedure introduced by Salter (Salter, A. *Conditioned Reflex Therapy*, 1949, Capricorn Books, New York) for increasing the social skills and lowering the anxiety level of unassertive individuals. Assertiveness is defined as a strong appropriate response to another human being that is neither submissive nor aggressive. Assertiveness is viewed as a way of participating in interpersonal relationships which reflects a healthy self-concept and high self-esteem without infringing on the rights of others" (Walrond-Skinner, 1986, p. 17).

ASSOCIATE/ASSOCIATION: The instruction given by a therapist after the patient has recounted a dream. He is asked to think about each person, place, and thing in the dream and to let pictures and memories float to the surface; he then shares these with the therapist. Associations help the therapist become more aware of the client's unconscious conflicts.

ATTENTION SPAN: "In popular terminology, the duration of an individual's attention to a single object or event" (Chaplin, 1975, p. 505).

BASELINE: The typical or average level of performance of a particular behavior (i.e., thought, action, physiological change, etc.) that is used as a point of comparison in assessing changes in that behavior (i.e., increase or decrease) after specific therapeutic interventions are employed.

BEHAVIOR THERAPY/BEHAVIOR MODIFICATION: "The systematic application of learning principles and techniques to the treatment of behavior disorders. Behavior therapists assume that disorders are learned ways of behaving that are maladaptive and consequently can best be modified in more adaptive directions through relearning. In contrast to traditional forms of psychotherapy, behavior therapy minimizes the client's verbal explorations toward the eventual restructuring of personality by removing repressions and achieving insight. Instead, a direct attack is made on the client's symptoms. Thus, if the client complains of anxiety, the behavior therapist does not attempt to trace the history of the problem back to childhood but instead initiates a program of reconditioning designed to alleviate the symptoms of anxiety in those situations in which the client finds them most troublesome" (Chaplin, 1975, p. 57).

BONDING: The term used by Winnicott et al to describe the crucial relationship between the mother and her infant consisting of accurate empathic nonverbal communication developed through touching, holding, staring at each other, imitation, and responsive interactions. Some researchers feel bonding is a biological need, like eating and breathing.

BOUNDARIES: *see also* ENMESHMENT, SEPARATION-INDIVIDUATION. Psychoanalysts frequently refer to unclear boundaries between a person and other people, ideas or objects resulting from inappropriate individuation in the pre-Oedipal period. A two-year-old spends a great deal of time sorting out what is "me" from what is "not me." Family therapists have discovered that many family conflicts are the result of the enmeshment caused by individuals who have inadequate ego boundaries.

BULIMIA: "Insatiable hunger; a type of eating disorder consisting of a pattern of eating binges during which a large amount of food is ingested in a short period of time (usually less than two hours). Each binge is typically followed with a depression in mood and disparaging self-criticism and, in some, imposition of a rigid diet. Bulimia occurs most frequently in females, beginning in adolescence or early adulthood, and extending over a period of many years" (Campbell, 1981, p. 91).

CHARACTERLOGICAL DISORDER: *see* PERSONALITY DISORDER.

CHILD: The term employed by Eric Berne to describe that consistent pattern of feeling, experience, and behavior of an individual (i.e., ego state) which is "an archaic relic from an early significant period of life" (Berne, 1966, p. 362).

CLIENT-CENTERED THERAPY: "A system of psychotherapy based on the assumption that the client or subject is in the best position to resolve his own problems provided that the therapist can establish a warm, permissive atmosphere in which the client feels free to discuss his problems and to obtain insight into them. In client-centered therapy, the therapist assumes a nondirective role; he does not advise, interpret, or intervene except to offer encouragement, and occasional restatements of the client's remarks for the purpose of emphasis and clarification" (Chaplin, 1975, p. 91).

COGNITION: "A general concept embracing all forms of knowing. It includes perceiving, imagining, reasoning, and judging" (Chaplin, 1975, p. 94).

COGNITIVE BEHAVIOR MODIFICATION/COGNITIVE BEHAVIOR THERAPY: "A set of principles and procedures developed chiefly by Meichenbaum (Meichenbaum, D. *Cognitive-Behavior Modification: An Integrative Approach*, 1977, Plenum Press, New York) and his colleagues. Meichenbaum's model is one of stimulus-response-reinforcement and is essentially an operant conditioning approach, with the patient's self-statements being regarded as discriminative stimuli. Approaches to cognitive behaviour therapy include self-instructional training, stress inoculation and coping skills interventions. Although cognitive behaviour therapy has some areas in common with Beck's cognitive therapy, notably its recognition of the importance of cognitive processes, it is also closely related to behavioural techniques and ideas" (Walrond-Skinner, 1986, p. 56).

COMPULSIVENESS: "The trait of repetitiveness in behavior often in a way that is inappropriate or contrary to the individual's inclinations. The trait or characteristic of rigidity and lack of flexibility in behaving" (Chaplin, 1975, p. 105).

COMPULSION: A strong, usually irresistible impulse to perform an act contrary to the will of the subject. "Compulsions are obsessions in action" (Chaplin, 1975, p. 109).

CONFLICT: "The simultaneous occurrence of two or more mutually antagonistic impulses or motives" (Chaplin, 1975, p. 109).

COUNTER TRANSFERENCE: Transference on the part of the analyst of the repressed feelings aroused by the patient.

CRISIS-INTERVENTION: "Psycho-social procedures offered to individuals, families or groups experiencing a state of crisis . . . . The minimum objective of all approaches to crisis intervention is 'the psychological resolution of the immediate crisis and restoration to at least the level of functioning that existed prior to the crisis' (Aquilea, D.C. and Messick, J.M. *Crisis Intervention: Theory and Methodology*, 1974, C.V. Mosby, St. Louis). Because the client may be in a state of shock, be exhausted or extremely depressed, the therapist is typically more active and directive when using crisis intervention compared with other forms of treatment. During the stage of acute stress, psychotropic drugs may be required and also expert advice and guidance. Intensive care may be needed for a short period and the client's responsibilities may have to be taken over. After the initial period of acute crisis has passed, therapeutic work should include the promotion of catharsis and the ventilation of feelings; facilitation of communication; identification of the problem and its various aspects; bolstering of the client's self-esteem and the facilitation of problem-solving behaviour. Crisis intervention embraces a variety of methods and arose in the USA out of a need to develop immediate, inexpensive, relevant and often non-medical sources of help" (Walrond-Skinner, 1986, pp. 85–86).

DAY-RESIDUE: "Remnants of experiences which play a part in determining the content of dreams" (Chaplin, 1975, p. 129).

DEFENSE MECHANISM: "Any behavior pattern which protects the psyche from anxiety, shame, or guilt. Some common defense mechanisms are: repression, regression, projection, identification, fantasy, compensation, sublimation, reaction-formation, and aggression" (Chaplin, 1975, p. 131).

DEFENSES: *see* DEFENSE MECHANISM.

DENIAL (an ego defense): "A primitive defense, consisting of an attempt to disavow the existence of unpleasant reality" (Campbell, 1981, p. 163).

DEPRESSION: "In the normal individual, a state of despondency characterized by feelings of inadequacy, lowered activity, and pessimism about the future. In pathological cases, an extreme state of unresponsiveness to stimuli, together with self-depreciation, delusions of inadequacy, and hopelessness" (Chaplin, 1975, p. 135).

DEVELOPMENTAL STAGE: "A period in the life of the individual in which specific traits or behavior patterns appear" (Chaplin, 1975, p. 140).

DEVELOPMENTAL TASK: "Skills, levels of achievement, and social adjustment which are considered important at certain ages for the successful adjustment of the individual" (Chaplin, 1975, p. 140).

DUAL PERSONALITY: *see also* MULTIPLE PERSONALITY. "A multiple personality consisting of two components" (Chaplin, 1975, p. 158).

DYADIC INTIMACY/DYADIC RELATIONSHIP: *see also* BONDING. An intimate relationship between two persons.

DYNAMIC PROBLEMS: Conflicts of an unconscious nature that cause maladaptive behaviors in an individual.

DYSLEXIA: An impairment in one's ability to read and/or one's ability to understand what is read.

EGO: "One of the three agencies which compose the structure of the psyche . . . . The ego is the central agency of the personality, whose task is to mediate the conflicting demands of the superego, the id and those of external reality . . . . The ego employs censorship to modify the instinctual drives and signals anxiety when the contents of the id threaten to overwhelm it, whilst its own defence mechanisms protect it from threat from the external world . . . . According to Freud, the ego develops gradually out of the id through having to adapt to the demands of external reality. It is built up through the introjection of part objects and object relations. Melanie Klein, however, conceives of the ego as existing embryonically from birth and of being capable of distinguishing the self from the object. And so, from the beginning it uses primitive defence mechanisms such as splitting and projection" (Walrond-Skinner, 1986, p. 108).

EMPATHY: "Putting oneself into the psychological frame of reference of another, so that the other person's thinking, feeling, and acting are understood and, to some extent, predictable. Carl Rogers defines empathy as the ability to accompany another wherever the other person's feelings lead him, no matter how strong, deep, destructive, or abnormal they may seem" (Campbell, 1981, p. 215).

ENMESHMENT: *see also* BONDING, SEPARATION-INDIVIDUATION. The state of psychological merging typical of that experienced by infants and mothers. An individual who is not able to achieve separation from his mother at the appropriate developmental stage remains attached to her, or her derivative (i.e., father, wife, job, money, jogging, bulimia, etc.).

EXISTENTIAL PSYCHOLOGY: *see* EXISTENTIAL PSYCHOTHERAPY.

EXISTENTIAL PSYCHOTHERAPY: "A trend within and an approach to psychotherapy, influenced by such existential philosophers as Kierkegaard, Heidegger and Sartre, and the phenomenology of Husserl. Existential psychotherapy arose out of a dissatisfaction with what was perceived to be the reductionist and mechanistic aspects of psychoanalysis. Instead, the idea of the individual's existence or capacity to 'stand out' or transcend self through self-consciousness and self-reflection is the fundamental idea behind this approach. Existential psychotherapists, who include Binswanger,

Boss, May and Laing, concern themselves with how the patient experiences life rather than with diagnosis or with understanding the causality of his problems. They emphasise the importance of the current and immediate moment of experience, and stress the importance of consciousness, personal identity, the unity of the person and the search for meaning in life" (Walrond-Skinner, 1986, p. 123).

EXTINGUISHED BEHAVIOR: *see also* REINFORCEMENT. Behavior which gradually diminishes and ultimately ceases due to the withdrawal of its reinforcement (i.e., reward). For example, if the cookie jar remains empty after the homemaker takes a job, the young man will eventually cease to remove the lid.

FAMILY DYNAMICS/FAMILY SYSTEM: The manner in which a family system is interrelated and how it interacts. A change in one part of the family system will cause changes in other parts of the family system.

FEAR: *see* ANXIETY.

FRAME OF REFERENCE: "A standard or attitude against which actions or results are judged" (Chaplin, 1975, p. 206).

FREE-FLOATING ANXIETY: *see also* ANXIETY. "Pervasive and chronic anxiety not attached to specific objects or situations" (Chaplin, 1975, p. 207).

GESTALT CHAIR TECHNIQUE: *see also* GESTALT THERAPY. A technique used by Gestalt therapists. The client sits across from an empty chair and is instructed by the therapist to enact "different aspects of himself, moving from one chair to another and conducting a dialogue between different aspects of the self" (Walrond-Skinner, 1986, p. 171).

GESTALT PSYCHOLOGY: "Literal German meaning 'form' or 'whole.' The Gestalt approach to psychology was developed in Germany during the 1930s and 1940s by Wertheimer, Kohler and Koffka based on the early work of the philosopher and psychologist von Ehrenfels. Their work sprang out of a dissatisfaction with psychoanalysis and behaviourism and the inability of these theories to deal with the person as a whole. In contrast, Gestalt psychologists suggest that the individual perceives and responds to configurations as wholes. Their ideas were influential in the development of humanistic psychology and found particular clinical expression in Gestalt therapy" (Walrond-Skinner, 1986, p. 152).

GESTALT THERAPY: *see also* GESTALT PSYCHOLOGY. "A method of therapy developed by Fritz Perls which stresses an a-historical, existential approach and which aims to help the individual to be self-supportive and self-responsible. The primary therapeutic tool is the development of awareness of what is going on within the self at any given moment . . . . The approach is holistic in that it is directed to the whole person in his environment. It draws upon the theoretical insights of Gestalt psychology and it has been influenced technically by both psychodrama and the body therapies. Gestalt therapy is practised in both the individual and the group work setting, although the group work approach is more usual" (Walrond-Skinner, 1986, p. 152).

GRIEF WORK: *see also* STAGES OF GRIEF. The therapeutic process by which strong feelings associated with loss and/or deprivation are resolved.

HAASS: *see also* HUMOR, ANTICIPATION, ALTRUISM, SUBLIMATION, SUPPRESSION (all are ego defenses). The acronym for the five most sophisticated defenses used to stay out of touch with unconscious conflicts. They are: humor, anticipation, altruism, sublimation, and suppression.

HUMANISTIC PSYCHOLOGY: "The group of approaches which stresses the need to engage the whole person in the psychotherapeutic endeavour. One of the major orientations to psychotherapy, the humanistic approach emphasises the future, in contrast to the past or present emphases of the psychoanalytic and behavioural orientations respectively. The group includes the work of Rogers, Maslow, Allport and Goldstein. They have some views in common with existential writers such as Tillich, Binswanger and Laing, and proponents of new forms of group and individual therapy such as Perls and Berne . . . .. The humanistic approaches emphasise relationship factors in therapy and are anti-technical. Experience and meaning are considered to be the important aspects of the patient's life, rather than overt behaviour, and these should be of primary concern to the therapist . . . . Humanistic psychologists view the therapeutic relationship as a participative endeavour between two human beings both of whom are seeking growth from the relationship. Goals include self-actualisation, personal growth, self-understanding and re-education . . . . Helping the client to clarify his values and beliefs is also an important task of therapy" (Walrond-Skinner, 1986, p. 172).

HUMOR (an ego defense): *see also* HAASS. One of the five "higher level defenses." "A pleasant, affable attitude" (Chaplin, 1975, p. 241) that encourages both oneself and others when meeting life's trials.

HYPERACTIVITY: "Manifestations of disturbed child behavior, indicating the child whose movements and actions are performed at a higher than normal rate of speed and/or the child who is constantly restless and in motion" (Campbell, 1981, p. 290).

ID: "One of the three agencies which between them compose the structure of the psyche, according to psychoanalytic theory. The id represents the major portion of the unconscious, although it is not co-terminus with it, since both t̲ ̲ ̰ ego and the superego have unconscious aspects . . . . Freud (Freud, S. 'The ego and the id'; *Standard Edition*, vol. 19, 1923, Hogarth Press, London) viewed the id as 'a chaos . . . filled with energy reaching it from the instincts. It has no organisation, produces no collective will but only a striving to bring about the satisfaction of instinctual needs subject to the observance of the pleasure principle.' In its lack of organisation and its complete unconsciousness it stands in contrast to both the ego and the superego . . . . Haman (Haman, A. 'What do we mean by id?'; *J. of Am. Psychoanalytic Assoc.*, 1969, vol. 17, pp. 353–380) suggests that the id is best understood as a way of acting that conforms to the infantile mode—irrational, unrestrained and heedless of consequences or contradictions. Such spontaneous action can either be aggressively egocentric or creatively part of lateral thinking and hence independent and novel in its results" (Walrond-Skinner, 1986, pp. 174–175).

IDEALIZATION (an ego defense): "Process or act of idealizing. Freud says that idealization is 'sexual over-estimation' of the love-object. It is 'the origin of the peculiar state of being in love'. Emphasis is placed upon the object rather than the aim. As Freud maintains, the love-object 'is aggrandized and exalted in the mind'" (Campbell, 1981, p. 303).

IDENTIFICATION (an ego defense): "A form of internalisation by which the individual can model aspects of his or her self upon others. According to Freud's later views, it is an important means by which the personality is formed and the ego and superego developed. The mechanism is of central importance in psychoanalysis and in understanding the way in which many psychotherapeutic processes operate" (Walrond-Skinner, 1986, p. 175).

IDENTIFICATION WITH THE AGGRESSOR: *see also* IDENTIFICATION. In situations of prolonged helplessness, while experiencing continuous or intermittent abuse, individuals often take on the values, beliefs, habits and physical mannerisms of the abuser. For example, concentration camp victims, when interviewed by researchers, sometimes believed they were inferior, should have been incarcerated, and that the Germans were a superior race justified to inflict torture and death. These individuals tried to carry themselves physically like their guards.

IDENTITY CRISIS: "Social role conflict as perceived by the person himself; loss of the sense of personal sameness and historical continuity, and/or inability to accept or adopt the role the person believes is expected of him by society. Identity crises are frequent in adolescence, when they appear to be triggered by the combination of sudden increase in the strength of drives with sudden changes in the role the adolescent is expected to adopt socially, educationally, or vocationally" (Campbell, 1981, p. 306).

INDIVIDUATION: *see* SEPARATION-INDIVIDUATION.

INFANTILE CONFLICTS: Conflicts characterized by immature, childlike behavior, projections, and/or feelings on the part of an adult or older child. Such conflicts typically involve significant dependency and separation-individuation issues.

INTELLECTUALIZATION (an ego defense): A defense mechanism in which a person analyzes a personal problem in strictly intellectual terms and excludes all feeling and emotion from consciousness. For example, a patient, when talking of the severe abuse he experienced as a child, discusses his family's structure and conflicts, but expresses no emotion when mentioning his father's abusiveness.

INTERNAL DYNAMICS: *see* DYNAMIC PROBLEMS.

INTERNALIZATION: "The incorporation of attitudes, standards of conduct, opinions, etc. within the personality. Freud believed that the superego, or moral aspect of personality, was derived from the internalization of parental attitudes" (Chaplin, 1975, p. 267).

INTERPERSONAL: "That which takes place between persons" and/or that which characterizes "processes which arise as a result of the interaction of individuals" (Chaplin, 1975, pp. 267-268).

INTERPRETATION: "The description or formulation of the meaning or significance of a patient's productions and, particularly, the translation into a form meaningful for the patient of his resistances and symbols and character defenses" (Campbell, 1981, p. 332). This is accomplished by the therapist who gains data for interpretation by observation of the patient and by examination of the patient's behavior, associations, feelings, and dreams.

INTRAPSYCHIC: "Taking place within the personality or mind, such as intrapsychic conflicts which are expressions of the existence of two opposing motivations or impulses within the individual" (Chaplin, 1975, p. 269).

JUNIOR: *see also* UNCONSCIOUS. A synonym for the unconscious coined by Agnes Sanford to personify the rebellious, unruly part of herself. "For what I want to do I do not do, but what I hate I do" (Romans 7:15).

LATENCY: The developmental stage "extending from the end of the infantile to the beginning of the adolescent stage. In point of years it normally begins at about the age of five and terminates at about the age of puberty" (Campbell, 1981, p. 348). During this period, the child stops being very concerned about his relationships with either parent and he invests energy into his own physical, mental and intellectual mastery of complex tasks.

LATENT CONTENT OF DREAMS: "The hidden content of a dream which must be brought out during analysis by means of free association. Presumably, some impulses and ideas are so incompatible with the individual's evaluation of himself they must be hidden or disguised even in dreams" (Chaplin, 1975, p. 283).

LIBIDINAL DRIVE: *see also* LIBIDO. In general, a person's sexual drive. Psychoanalysis "takes as its point of departure the concept of the libido, which is defined basically as sexual energy, both in its original form and as it is modified during development into all forms of love, affection and the will to live" (Chaplin, 1975, p. 416).

LIBIDO: *see also* LIBIDINAL DRIVE. "In psychoanalysis, the energy of the sexual drive; but because Freud's consideration of the death or destructive drive came relatively late in the development of his psychology, the term libido is commonly used in a more general sense to refer also to the energy of the death or aggressive drive" (Campbell, 1981, pp. 352–353).

LONG-TERM DYNAMIC PERSONALITY RECONSTRUCTION: Developmental stages which were not properly traversed by the patient at the appropriate age can be reworked through the therapeutic relationship resulting in psychological maturity. Inappropriate defenses, inaccurate perceptions, acting-out behavior, etc. can be replaced by synthetic (i.e., man-made) ego functions.

LONG-TERM DYNAMIC PSYCHOTHERAPY: *see also* LONG-TERM DYNAMIC PERSONALITY RECONSTRUCTION. The reconstruction of a patient's personality requires skillful interventions by the therapist on a regular basis. These interventions are based on extensive knowledge of the unconscious, normal and abnormal development, defenses, and an acquired empathic resonance with the patient.

LOVE-OBJECT: That person or thing to which a portion of an individual's libidinal energy is attached.

MANIFEST CONTENT OF DREAMS: "Content of the dream as it is experienced by the dreamer. This aspect of the dream is of far less significance than the latent content" (Chaplin, 1975, p. 299).

MEDICAL-DISEASE MODEL: "The conceptualization of behavior disorders and psychological abnormalities as diseases analogous to organic diseases" (Chaplin, 1975, p. 308).

MIRRORING/MIRRORING MOTHER: The reactions of the mother inform the infant about himself. Her smiles, frowns, words, touches, gestures give him a sense of his value and capacity. The first sense of himself, his body image, comes from how he is physically handled long before he can purposefully move himself.

MODELING: "Learning to make a response by watching another make that response. Imitation" (Chaplin, 1975, p. 322).

MOOD-SWINGS: "The oscillation between periods of the feeling of well-being and those of depression or 'blueness'. All people have mood-swings, blue hours, or blue days. Mood-swings are somewhat more marked in the neurotic than in the normal. In the manic-depressive patient, the swings are of much greater intensity and much longer duration" (Campbell, 1981, p. 393).

MULTIPLE PERSONALITY: "A pathological condition in which the integrated personality fragments into two or more personalities each of which manifests a relatively complete integration of its own and which is relatively independent of the other personalities" (Chaplin, 1975, p. 329).

NEUROSIS: *see also* NEUROTIC PATTERNS. "The group of functional nervous or mental disorders, less serious and less fundamental than psychoses" (Drever, 1972, p. 233).

NEUROTIC PATTERNS: "The self-perpetuating and self-defeating behaviour that occurs in repeated dysfunctional behaviour even when the patient is conscious of its destructive consequences to himself and/or others" (Walrond-Skinner, 1986, p. 231).

OBSESSION: "An idea, emotion, or impulse that repetitively and insistently forces itself into consciousness even though it is unwelcome. An obsession may be regarded as essentially normal when it does not interfere substantially with thinking or other mental functions; such an obsession is short-lived and can usually be minimized or nullified by diverting attention to other topics. Morbid or pathological obsessions, in contrast, tend to be long-lived and may constitute a never-ending harrassment of mental functioning; they are but little subject to conscious control and force the sufferer into all sorts of maneuvers in his vain attempt to rid himself of the thoughts. Most commonly, obsessions appear as ideas, or sensory images, which are strongly charged with emotions" (Campbell, 1981, pp. 423–424).

OBSESSIVE PERSONALITY: *see also* OBSESSION. A person who suffers from frequent, intense, and chronic obsessions.

ORIGINAL ENMESHED UNION: *see also* BONDING. The relationship that develops between a mother (or mother substitute) and her infant. It is marked by the infant's total dependence upon his mother for physical survival and emotional nurture.

PAIN-PLACE: The term used by Fritz Perls, the founder of Gestalt therapy, to describe the core of the problem of a patient. The pain-place lies below the repression barrier. The goal of the therapist is to assist the patient in breaking through the repression barrier to deal with his core problem(s) in a therapeutic manner.

PANIC: An experience or attack of overwhelming anxiety which is often accompanied by feelings of intense apprehension, fear, terror, or impending doom.

PARANOID PROJECTIONS: Attitudes, traits, ideas, or impulses attributed to another by a person who, in fact, harbors these characteristics and cannot accept them as within himself. Such a person is typically hypersensitive, rigid, suspicious, and has a tendency to blame others.

PARENT: The term employed by Eric Berne to describe that consistent pattern of feeling, experience, and behavior of an individual (i.e., ego state) that is "borrowed from a parental figure" and "may exert itself as an indirect influence, or be directly exhibited in parental behavior" (Berne, 1966, p. 366).

PASSIVE-AGGRESSIVE CHARACTERLOGICAL STRUCTURE/PASSIVE-AGGRESSIVE PERSONALITY DISORDER: A personality configuration marked by "a pervasive pattern of passive resistance to demands for adequate social and occupational performance, beginning by early adulthood and present in a variety of contexts. The resistance is expressed indirectly rather than directly, and results in pervasive and persistent social and occupational ineffectiveness even when more self-assertive and effective behavior is possible. The name of the disorder is based on the assumption that such people are passively expressing covert aggression. People with this disorder habitually resent and oppose demands to increase or maintain a given level of functioning . . . . The resistance is expressed indirectly through such maneuvers as procrastination, dawdling, stubbornness, intentional inefficiency, and 'forgetfulness' . . . . These people become sulky, irritable, or argumentative when asked to do something they do not want to do. They often protest to others about how unreasonable the demands being made on them are, and resent useful suggestions from others concerning how to be more productive" (*Diagnostic and Statistical Manual of Mental Disorders [Third Edition-Revised]*, 1987, pp. 356–357).

PERSEVERATION (an ego defense): "A tendency to continue an ongoing activity even when it becomes inappropriate" (Chaplin, 1975, p. 380). The activity may encompass both physical actions and speech.

PERSONALITY DISORDER: "Personality is a set of relatively stable, predictable, and ego-syntonic [i.e., ego acceptable] habits that characterize the person in his way of managing day-to-day living; when those habits are enough beyond the normal range to warrant the appellation of personality disorder is difficult to define, and often the label is more a social diagnosis of nonconformity than a designation of disease process in the usual sense. In general, however, what are termed personality disorders are patterns of relating to the environment that are so rigid, fixed and immutable as to limit severely the likelihood of effective functioning or satisfying interpersonal relationships" (Campbell, 1981, p. 457).

PHOBIA/PHOBIC REACTION: "A strong, persistent and irrational fear which is elicited by a specific stimulus or situation, such as a morbid fear of closed places" (i.e., claustrophobia) (Chaplin, 1975, p. 385).

POSTPARTUM DEPRESSION: *see also* DEPRESSION. A state of depression that occurs in some women after childbirth.

PRE-OEDIPAL: "Pertaining to the stage of development before the onset of the Oedipus complex, or the child's sexual attraction for the parent of the opposite sex" (Chaplin, 1975, p. 402); it extends from birth to approximately thirty-six months of age.

PRIMAL SCREAM: The release of "repressed, painful feelings about the many needs of childhood" through a therapeutic process (i.e., primal therapy) that encourages "kicking, screaming, crying, and shouting." Primal therapy was developed by Janov and is based on Otto Rank's work on birth trauma (Walrond-Skinner, 1986, pp. 263–264).

PRIMITIVE EMOTIONS/PRIMITIVE FEELINGS: Emotions which pertain to the earliest stages of human development (i.e., infancy).

PSYCHOANALYSIS: "A system of psychology directed toward the understanding, cure, and prevention of mental disorders. As conceived by Sigmund Freud, psychoanalysis is a dynamic system of psychology which seeks the roots of human behavior in unconscious motivation and conflict. It takes as its point of departure the concept of the libido, which is defined basically as sexual energy, both in its original form and as it is modified during development into all forms of love, affection, and the will to live" (Chaplin, 1975, p. 416).

PSYCHOLOGICALLY UNAVAILABLE: A term used to describe an individual who is defensive, rigid, and resistant to the therapeutic process. Such individuals do not voluntarily seek professional psychological assistance. If they do involve themselves in psychotherapy, they generally terminate therapy prematurely.

PSYCHOSIS: "A severe mental disorder characterized by disorganization of the thought processes, disturbances in emotionality, disorientation as to time, space, and person, and, in some cases, hallucinations and delusions" (Chaplin, 1975, p. 431).

RAPPROCHEMENT PERIOD: see also SEPARATION-INDIVIDUATION. One of the four subphases of the separation-individuation process as postulated by Margaret Mahler. Rapprochement is the "active approach toward the mother (by the walking infant), replacing the relative obliviousness to her that prevailed during the practicing period" (of walking) (Campbell, 1981, p. 579). This subphase occurs from approximately eighteen months to thirty-six months of age.

RATIONAL EMOTIVE THERAPY: See COGNITIVE THERAPY.

RATIONALIZATION (an ego defense): "A defence mechanism whereby the individual seeks to 'explain' to himself and others behaviour, motives, attitudes, thoughts, or feelings which are otherwise unacceptable . . . . For example, racial prejudice may be rationalised by an appeal to the greater good, which can be achieved by all races if 'separate development' is promoted" (Walrond-Skinner, 1986, p. 286).

REACTION-FORMATION (an ego defense): The development in one's ego of certain conscious, socially acceptable traits and attitudes that are the opposite of early and unsocialized traits which reside in one's unconscious. It is "a form of defense against urges that are unacceptable to the ego" and "it is one of the earliest of the defense-mechanisms and one of the most fragile" (Campbell, 1981, p. 533). For example, the aggressive Marine who is defending against internal cowardice.

RECONSTRUCTION: "The interpretation of psychoanalytic data so as to illuminate the past development of personality and the present meaning of the material for the individual" (Chaplin, 1975, p. 446).

REINFORCEMENT: A reward that strengthens or increases the frequency of a particular behavior. For example, money is a reinforcement for work.

REM SLEEP: A stage of sleep characterized by rapid eye movement (i.e., REM) in which dreaming occurs. It averages two hours a night, divided into seven segments.

REPARENTING: A term used by humanistic psychologists to identify the process through which conflicts stemming from childhood are alleviated through the relationship with the therapist. Existential insights replace dynamic interpretations and self disclosure for congruence replaces the analytic "white-sheet" stance of the therapist doing long-term personality reconstruction. However, both techniques depend on an empathic relationship producing corrective emotional experiences.

REPETITION COMPULSION (an ego defense): "The tendency unconsciously to repeat painful experiences. It is sometimes viewed as a destructive urge, such as the repeated choice of a violent marital partner, and Freud used the idea in support of his concept of death instinct. It can also be viewed as an effort on the part of the ego to recreate a situation in order to resolve it. Freud's 'new editions of old conflicts,' transferred on to the relationship with the analyst, is an example of the positive aspect of repetition compulsion" (Walrond-Skinner, 1986, p. 297).

REPRESSION (an ego defense): "The forceful ejection from consciousness of impulses, memories, or experiences that are painful or shameful and generate a high level of anxiety. Repression, according to Freudian psychoanalysis, is a function of the ego" (Chaplin, 1975, p. 454) and "like all defence mechanisms, it is itself an unconscious process" (Walrond-Skinner, 1986, pp. 297–298). For example, most people repress their murderous rage at a parent who punishes them unfairly.

REPRESSION BARRIER: The conscious ego is defended from ongoing inevitable unconscious conflicts between the superego and the id (parent and child) by the repression barrier. It contains the defenses used to keep the individual unaware so he can attend to managing his daily affairs in the world. The repression barrier has affective and cognitive components.

ROGERIAN THERAPY: *see* CLIENT-CENTERED THERAPY.

SCHIZOPHRENIA: *see also* PSYCHOSIS. "A general name for a group of psychotic reactions characterized by withdrawal, disturbances in emotional and affective life, and depending upon the type, the presence of hallucinations, delusions, negativistic behavior, and progressive deterioration" (Chaplin, 1975, p. 471).

SELF-ACTUALIZATION: "The innate capacity of human beings to grow and develop towards emotional and psychological maturity. The term is used by most humanistic therapists to describe the central motivating tendency in life" (Walrond-Skinner, 1986, p. 307).

SELF-SOOTHE: The ability to comfort and nurture oneself (e.g., to choose to listen to soothing music when feeling stressed by the day's events).

SELF-STIMULATE: The ability to energize oneself to meet one's needs (e.g., to choose to take a walk in order to change a bad mood).

SEPARATION-ENMESHMENT CRISIS: *see* SEPARATION-INDIVIDUATION.

Separation-Individuation: "A phase in the mother-child relationship during which the child begins to perceive himself as distinct from the mother and develops a sense of individual identity and an image of the self as an object. This stage begins at the time the child can walk and thus separate himself physically from the mother, at about 18 months of age, immediately following the symbiotic stage" (Campbell, 1981, p. 579). Persons who have experienced a poor bonding relationship with their mother or mother-surrogate will experience serious problems with separation-individuation and frequently re-enact separation, individuation and rapprochement issues in their adult relationships.

Short-Term Dynamic Expressive Psychotherapy: "A method of treatment in which the therapist's dominant aim is to encourage and help the patient to bring out, verbalize, act out, or emotionally express all ideas and feelings so that both the patient and the therapist come to know the dynamic emotional roots of the patient's symptoms and illness. Through encouragement and by bringing about a reversal of the covering up (or normal) defensive mechanism, expressive therapy endeavors to uncover the roots of mental emotional illness. As epitomized in psychoanalysis, the main purpose of expressive therapy is, through a reversal of the repressive defense mechanisms, to shift the material from the unconscious realm into the realm of conscious thought" (Campbell, 1981, pp. 648–649). "Short-term" refers to the duration of the treatment. Short-term therapy is more suitable with less disturbed persons, with its focus being on specific symptoms and/or problem areas.

Short-Term Supportive Psychotherapy: "Supportive therapy consists of encouraging or promoting the development of maximal, optimal use of the patient's assets; its objectives are to strengthen existing defenses, elaborate better mechanisms to maintain control, and restore to an adaptive equilibrium. Included in supportive therapy are guidance, environmental manipulation, externalization of interests, reassurance, pressure, . . . persuasion, catharsis, and desensitization" (Campbell, 1981, p. 520). Typically, short-term therapy lasts not more than 20 sessions and is oriented toward problem-solving. Short-term therapy is also focused, circumscribed, and action-oriented.

Somatization (an ego defense): A process in which an individual expresses his psychic conflicts in physical manifestations. For example, an individual who is fearful of performing in a recital develops a severe headache that is so intense, he is unable to perform.

Stages of Grief: The five stages of grief as described by Kübler-Ross (Kübler-Ross, E. *On Death and Dying*, 1970, Tavistock, London): denial, anger, bargaining, depression, and acceptance.

Sublimation (an ego defense): *see also* HAASS. One of the five "higher level defenses." Sublimation means putting energy into areas other than those we cannot change. It involves disengaging from hopeless tasks and engaging in productive activities.

Superego: That part of the psychic apparatus which mediates between ego drives and social ideals, acting as a conscience that may be partly conscious and partly unconscious.

SUPPORTIVE INTROJECT: The therapist or significant other to whom a patient attributes parentlike importance and thus incorporates the attitudes of this supportive person as his own. More specifically, introjection is "a form of internalisation by which objects, feelings and situations are transposed from the outside world into the person's internal world . . . . The purpose of introjection is to keep the self in contact with important objects when physically separated from them. This also protects the ego from anxiety, either by bringing into it good objects, to strengthen it against the outside world, or lost objects which can thus be retrieved and retained forever . . . . Conversely, the introjection of 'bad' objects allows the ego to possess them and thereby control them" (Walrond-Skinner, 1986, p. 191).

SUPPRESSION (an ego defense): *see also* HAASS. One of the five "higher level defenses" employed by a person to handle stressful life-situations. Suppression means not thinking about difficulties we are circumstantially unable to resolve.

THERAPEUTIC ALLIANCE: "The creation of a working relationship between therapist and patient. Prior to engaging in any change interventions, the therapist needs to gain the co-operation of the patient and overcome his resistance to treatment . . . . The term implies that each party is conscious of entering into a particular kind of relationship in order to achieve mutually agreed (upon) goals and that some sort of contract of work is either explicitly or implicitly made . . . . The quality of the therapeutic alliance appears to be a highly significant indicator of good prognosis. Premature termination or severe dependency on the therapist are both indicators that a good therapeutic alliance has not been achieved" (Walrond-Skinner, 1986, pp. 352–353).

TIME OUT: A technique used in behavior therapy, in which a client (typically a child) is temporarily removed from a positively reinforcing (i.e., rewarding) situation when he exhibits specific undesirable behavior, thereby decreasing such behavior. "It usually takes the form of removing the child for a brief period of time to his bedroom or other socially isolating environment . . . . Time out differs from the frequently used parental practice of sending the child to his room when the parent's patience is exhausted. First, time out is not imposed in anger but as an automatic consequence of the occurrence of particular behaviours. Second, time out is terminated when the behaviour stops so that appropriate behaviour is reinforced. Third, after the cessation of time out, there are no further consequences for the child such as recriminations or complaints about the behaviour which has caused the time out" (Walrond-Skinner, 1986, p. 358).

TRANSACTIONAL ANALYSIS: *see also* PARENT, ADULT, CHILD. "A theory of personality and a method of psychotherapy . . . . based on the concept of the individual's ego states (i.e., Parent, Adult, Child), structured analysis and the games and scripts which are used as a defence against the demands of external reality. The term transactional analysis, although usually employed as a generic term to describe a method of psychotherapy, is more properly reserved for the analysis of transactions which occur between two or more individuals. Used in this latter sense, it is a technique within the generic method, alongside script analysis, games analysis and the structural analysis of the ego states" (Walrond-Skinner, 1986, p. 364).

TRANSFERENCE: "The process whereby the patient displaces on to the therapist feelings, attitudes and attributes which properly belong to a significant attachment figure of the past, usually a parent, and responds to the therapist accordingly. Transference also refers to everything that is experienced in relation to the treatment arising from the unconscious phantasies that develop within the patient-therapist relationship. More widely, the term refers to the tendency to transfer on to any current relationship feelings and emotions that properly belong to a relationship with the past. To a greater or lesser extent, transference colours the real relationships of the present. In its specific sense, the understanding and resolution of transference is an essential ingredient of all psychoanalytic therapies" (Walrond-Skinner, 1986, pp. 364–365).

TRANSITIONAL OBJECT: "A term introduced by D.W. Winnicott to describe the infant's first possession and the way in which he or she uses it to develop in understanding from subjective experience based on infantile omnipotence to that which is objectively perceived through acknowledging a separate external world. Winnicott suggests that the baby negotiates the 'transitional' or intermediate phase between primary narcissism and object relations by becoming attached to a material possession such as a piece of blanket, rag or other soft object. The transitional object has in the child's possession the paradoxical quality of being 'me' and 'not me' at the same time. It acts as a defence against annihilation anxiety and is especially important to the child at bedtime, when lonely, or during periods of regression to an earlier phase of development. Winnicott suggests that the transitional object starts to be used between four and twelve months and may continue during the first few years of life. The use of transitional objects is a normal part of psychic growth and development" (Walrond-Skinner, 1986, pp. 367–368).

TRIANGULATION: "The process whereby a dyadic sub-system draws in a third party as a means of diffusing conflict between the pair. The process is described by Minuchin . . . and by Bowen, but is used widely by many writers on systems and family therapy. It occurs between family members such as the parental sub-system's triangulation of a child, parent or lover, and can be regarded as a systematic defence against conflict resolution. Where the third party is a child, one parent will side with the child against the other parent, so that both the triangulated child and the excluded parent experience intense stress . . . . Triangulation also occurs between the family and an outside helper, whereby the therapist, for example, is triangulated into a marital sub-system and used as a homeostatic regulator instead of an agent of change. This type of triangulation is an ingredient in most systems therapy, although it is particularly potent and obvious in conjoint marital therapy where the therapeutic system is literally a triangle" (Walrond-Skinner, 1986, p. 370).

UNCONSCIOUS: *see also* JUNIOR. "The term is used both as an adjective and as a noun in psychoanalytic theory. Used adjectively, the term is a description applied to certain mental contents which are not currently within the individual's consciousness. These include both the contents of the pre-conscious and the system unconscious. Used as a noun, the term refers to the system unconscious, the region of the mind which remains unavailable to the individual, until it emerges into consciousness through certain products (dreams), processes (word associations, free association and parapraxes), or behaviours (symptoms) . . . . For psychoanalytic therapists, the root to understanding and treating psychological problems lies through the unconscious and symptoms are viewed as conscious manifestations of unconscious conflicts" (Walrond-Skinner, 1986, pp. 372–373).

Glossary References

American Psychiatric Association. *Diagnostic and Statistical Manual of Mental Disorders (Third Edition —Revised)*. American Psychiatric Association, Washington, DC. 1987.

Berne, Eric. *Group Treatment*. Grove Press, Inc., New York. 1966.

Campbell, Robert Jean. *Psychiatric Dictionary—Fifth Edition*. Oxford University Press, New York & Oxford. 1981.

Chaplin, J.P. *Dictionary of Psychology—Revised Edition*. Dell Publishing Co., Inc., New York. 1975.

Drever, James. *A Dictionary of Psychology*. Penguin Books, Baltimore. 1972.

Walrond-Skinner, Sue. *A Dictionary of Psychotherapy*. Routledge & Kegan Paul, London & New York. 1986.

Appendix C

BIBLIOGRAPHY

Anonymous. *Prayer of a Confederate Soldier.*

Berne, E. *Transactional Analysis in Psychotherapy.* New York: Grove Press, 1961.

———. *Games People Play.* New York: Grove Press, 1964.

Bowen, M. *Family Therapy in Clinical Practice.* New York: Jason Aronson, 1978.

Bowlby, J. *Attachment and Loss Volume I: Attachment.* New York: Basic Books, 1969; second ed., 1982.

———. *Attachment and Loss Volume II: Separation: Anxiety and Anger.* New York: Basic Books, 1973.

———. *Attachment and Loss Volume III: Loss: Sadness and Depression.* New York: Basic Books, 1980.

Chambers, Oswald. *The Golden Book of Oswald Chambers: My Utmost for His Highest (Selections for the Year).* London: Simpkin Marshall, Ltd., 1927.

Coles, Robert. *The Privileged Ones: The Well-off and the Rich In America (Volume V of Children of Crisis).* Boston: Atlantic-Little, Brown Books, 1977.

Dowling, Colette. *The Cinderella Complex.* New York: Pocket Books, 1981.

Ellis, A. and Grieger, R. *Handbook of Rational-Emotive Therapy.* New York: Springer, 1977.

Erikson, E.H. *Childhood and Society (Second Edition).* New York: Norton, 1950, 1963.

Finch, J.G. "The Message of Anxiety." In *A Christian Existential Psychology: The Contributions of John G. Finch* (Malony, H.N., ed.). Lanham, Maryland: University Press of America, 1980.

Freud, S. "The Interpretation of Dreams (First Part)." In *The Standard Edition of the Complete Psychological Works of Sigmund Freud, Volume IV (1900)* [Strachey, J., trans. & ed.]. London: Hogarth Press and The Institute of Psycho-Analysis, 1953.

————. "The Interpretation of Dreams (Second Part) and On Dreams." In *The Standard Edition of the Complete Psychological Works of Sigmund Freud, Volume V (1900–1901)* [Strachey, J., trans. & ed.]. London: Hogarth Press and The Institute of Psycho-Analysis, 1953.

————. "The Ego and the Id and Other Works." In *The Standard Edition of the Complete Psychological Works of Sigmund Freud, Volume XIX (1923–1925)* [Strachey, J., trans. & ed.]. London: Hogarth Press and The Institute of Psycho-Analysis, 1961.

————. "Introductory Lectures on Psycho-Analysis (Parts I and II)." In *The Standard Edition of the Complete Psychological Works of Sigmund Freud, Volume XV (1915–1916)* [Strachey, J., trans. & ed.]. London: Hogarth Press and The Institute of Psycho-Analysis, 1963.

————. "Introductory Lectures on Psycho-Analysis (Part III)." In *The Standard Edition of the Complete Psychological Works of Sigmund Freud, Volume XVI (1916–1917)* [Strachey, J., trans. & ed.]. London: Hogarth Press and The Institute of Psycho-Analysis, 1963.

————. "New Introductory Lectures on Psycho-Analysis and Other Works." In *The Standard Edition of the Complete Psychological Works of Sigmund Freud, Volume XXII (1932–1936)* [Strachey, J., trans. & ed.]. London: Hogarth Press and The Institute of Psycho-Analysis, 1964.

Hansel, Tim. *Holy Sweat.* Waco, Texas: Word Books, 1987.

Hodges, Andrew G. *Jesus: An Interview Across Time: A Psychiatrist Looks at HIS Humanity.* Birmingham, Alabama: Village House Publishers, 1986.

Holy Bible: King James Version. Glasgow: William Collins, Sons and Company, Ltd., 1949; Philadelphia: The Westminster Book Stores, 1949.

Horney, K. *Neurosis and Human Growth.* New York: Norton, 1950.

Janov, A. *The Primal Scream.* New York: Delta, 1970.

Jones, Warren L. Personal communication, an unpublished manuscript. Pasadena, California, 1988.

Kierkegaard, Soren. *Fear and Trembling* and *The Sickness Unto Death* (Lowrie, W., trans.). Princeton: Princeton University Press, 1941, 1954.

————. *The Concept of Dread* (Lowrie, W., trans.). Princeton: Princeton University Press, 1944, 1957.

Klein, M. "The Development of the Child" (1921). In *Contributions to Psychoanalysis, 1921–1945.* London: Hogarth Press, 1948.

Kohut, H. *The Analysis of the Self.* New York: International Universities Press, 1971.

————. *The Restoration of the Self.* New York: International Universities Press, 1977.

Kübler-Ross, E. *On Death and Dying.* New York: Macmillan Publishing Company, Inc., 1969.

————. *Death: The Final Stage of Growth.* Englewood Cliffs: Prentice-Hall, 1975.

L'Engle, Madeleine. *A Wrinkle In Time.* New York: Dell Publishing Company, Inc., 1962.

————. *A Wind In The Door.* New York: Dell Publishing Company, Inc., 1973.

————. *A Swiftly Tilting Planet.* New York: Dell Publishing Company, Inc., 1978.

————. *Many Waters.* New York: Dell Publishing Company, Inc., 1986.

Lewis, C.S. *Mere Christianity*. New York: Macmillan Publishing Company, Inc., 1943, 1945, 1952.

——. *Perelandra*. New York: Macmillan Publishing Company, Inc., 1944.

——. *That Hideous Strength*. New York: Macmillan Publishing Company, Inc., 1944.

——. *The Great Divorce*. New York: Macmillan Publishing Company, Inc., 1946.

——. *The Abolition of Man*. New York: Macmillan Publishing Company, Inc., 1947.

——. *Miracles*. New York: Macmillan Publishing Company, Inc., 1947, 1960.

——. *A Grief Observed*. New York: The Seabury Press, 1961.

——. *The Problem of Pain*. New York: Macmillan Publishing Company, Inc., 1962.

——. *Out of the Silent Planet*. New York: Macmillan Publishing Company, Inc., 1965.

——. *The Screwtape Letters (Revised Edition)*. New York: Macmillan Publishing Company, Inc., 1982.

Liedloff, Jean. *The Continuum Concept*. Menlo Park: Addison-Wesley Publishing Company, Inc., 1975; revised ed., 1977.

Lowen, A. *Bioenergetics*. New York: Penguin Books, 1976.

Madame Guyon. *Madame Guyon's Spiritual Letters* (Edwards, G., comp. & ed.). Augusta, Maine: Christian Books Publishing House, 1982.

Mahler, M. *On Human Symbiosis and the Vicissitudes of Individuation, Vol. I: Infantile Psychosis*. New York: International Universities Press, 1968.

Mahler, M., Bergman, A. and Pine, F. *The Psychological Birth of the Human Infant: Symbiosis and Individuation*. New York: Basic Books, 1975.

Marx, Karl and Engels, Friedrich. "The Communist Manifesto." In *The Marxist Reader: The Most Significant and Enduring Works of Marxism* (Burns, E., commentary and notes). New York: Avenel Books, 1982.

Maslow, A. *Toward a Psychology of Being (Revised Edition)*. New York: Von Nostrand Reinhold, 1968.

May, R. *Psychology and the Human Dilemma*. New York: Van Nostrand Reinhold, 1967.

McNamara, William. *Christian Mysticism: A Psychology*. Chicago: Franciscan Herald Press, 1981.

Miller, A. *The Drama of the Gifted Child: How Narcissistic Parents Form and Deform the Emotional Lives of Their Talented Children* (Ward, R., trans.). New York: Basic Books, 1981.

Minuchin, S. *Families and Family Therapy*. Cambridge: Harvard University Press, 1974.

Mother Teresa of Calcutta. *Life in the Spirit: Reflections, Meditations, Prayers* (Spink, K., ed.). San Francisco: Harper and Row, 1983.

——. *Mother Teresa: Contemplative in the Heart of the World* (Scolozzi, A.D., ed.). Ann Arbor, Michigan: Servant Books, 1985.

Peck, M. Scott. *The Road Less Traveled: A New Psychology of Love, Traditional Values and Spiritual Growth*. New York: Simon and Schuster, 1978.

——. *People of the Lie: The Hope for Healing Human Evil*. New York: Simon and Schuster, 1983.

Peterson, Eugene H. *A Long Obedience in the Same Direction: Discipleship in an Instant Society.* Downers Grove, Illinois: InterVarsity Press, 1980.
———. *Traveling Light: Reflections on the Free Life.* Downers Grove, Illinois: Intervarsity Press, 1982.
Perls, F.S. *Gestalt Therapy Verbatim.* Lafayette, California: Real People Press, 1969.
Reich, W. *The Function of the Orgasm.* New York: Bantam Books, 1967.
Rogers, C. *Client-Centered Therapy.* Boston: Houghton Mifflin, 1951.
———. *On Becoming a Person.* Boston: Houghton Mifflin, 1961.
———. *Freedom to Learn.* Columbus: Merrill, 1969.
Saint Augustine. *Confessions* (Pine-Coffin, R.S., trans.). Baltimore: Penguin Books, 1961.
Sanford, Agnes. *The Healing Light.* Saint Paul, Minnesota: Macalester Park Publishing Company, 1947; revised ed., 1972.
———. *Behold Your God.* Saint Paul, Minnesota: Macalester Park Publishing Company, 1958.
Satir, V. *Conjoint Family Therapy: A Guide to Theory and Technique (Revised Edition).* Palo Alto: Science and Behavior Books, 1967.
Shoemaker, Samuel M. *Revive Thy Church Beginning with Me.* New York: Harper and Row, 1948.
———. *How to Become a Christian.* New York: Harper and Row, 1953.
———. *. . . . And Thy Neighbor.* Waco, Texas: Word Books, 1967.
Skinner, B.F. *Beyond Freedom and Dignity.* New York: Alfred A. Knopf, 1971.
Spitz, R.A. "Hospitalism: An Inquiry into the Genesis of Psychiatric Conditions in Early Childhood." In *The Psychoanalytic Study of the Child, Volume I.* New York: International Universities Press, 1945.
———. "Hospitalism: A Follow-up Report on Investigation Described in Volume I, 1945." In *The Psychoanalytic Study of the Child, Volume II.* New York: International Universities Press, 1946.
——— and Wolf, M. "Anaclitic Depression: An Inquiry into the Genesis of Psychiatric Conditions in Early Childhood, II." In *The Psychoanalytic Study of the Child, Volume II.* New York: International Universities Press, 1946.
———. *The First Year of Life.* New York: International Universities Press, 1965.
Stott, John R.W. *Basic Christianity (New Revised Version).* Grand Rapids: William B. Eerdmans Publishing Company, 1958, 1971, 1972.
Stringfellow, William. *A Second Birthday.* Garden City, New York: Doubleday & Company, Inc., 1970.
———. *A Simplicity of Faith: My Experience in Mourning.* Nashville: Abingdon, 1982.
Sullivan, H.S. *Interpersonal Theory of Psychiatry.* New York: Norton, 1953.
Ten Boom, Corrie. *Father Ten Boom: God's Man.* Old Tappan, New Jersey: Fleming H. Revell Company, 1971, 1973.
——— and Buckingham, Jamie. *Tramp for the Lord.* Old Tappan, New Jersey: Fleming H. Revell Company, 1974.
——— with Sherrill, John and Elizabeth. *The Hiding Place.* New York: Bantam Books, 1971.
———. *Don't Wrestle, Just Nestle (Jesus Is Victor Series).* Old Tappan, New Jersey: Fleming H. Revell Company, 1978.

Thompson Chain-Reference Bible: New International Version. Indianapolis: B.B. Kirkbride Bible Company, Inc. & Grand Rapids: The Zondervan Corporation, 1983.

Tournier, Paul. *The Meaning of Gifts* (Gilmour, J.S., trans.). Richmond, Virginia: John Knox Press, 1963.

Watson, J.B. *Behaviorism.* New York: Norton, 1925; revised ed., 1930.

Winnicott, D.W. *The Child, the Family, and the Outside World.* New York: Penguin Books, 1964.

―――. *The Maturational Processes and the Facilitating Environment: Studies In the Theory of Emotional Development.* New York: International Universities Press, 1965.

―――. *Playing and Reality.* New York: Basic Books, 1971.

Whitaker, C.A. and Napier, A.Y. *The Family Crucible.* New York: Harper and Row, 1978.

Whitaker, C.A. and Bumberry, W.M. *Dancing with the Family: A Symbolic-Experimental Approach.* New York: Bruner/Mazel, 1988.

Wordsworth, William. "The World Is Too Much With Us." In *Poems of William Wordsworth.* Wimbish Village near Saffron Walden/Essex, England: Collection Chosen & Published by Geoffrey Parker, 1969.